THE SCIENTIFIC PROOF OF CAUSAL REINCARNATION

A revelation of the fundamental truth of life and the universe

Dr. Zhong Maosen
(Venerable Ding Hong)

Translated by
Mahayana Pureland Team

ISBN Paperback: 9798511446448

Proofing: Proofed to Perfection
Cover Design: Creative Publishing Book Design
Interior Formatting and Design: Word 2 Kindle

Published by Mahayana Pureland Organization
www.mahayanapureland.org
Email: team@mahayanapureland.org

Dedicated to The Awakening of All Sentient Beings

This book is meant to benefit oneself and others.
By passing it on to the next person with affinity after
finishing reading, it is the practice of "giving"
and an act of "saving the planet."

TABLE OF CONTENTS

Preface ix

About Dr. Zhong Maosen (Venerable Ding Hong) xiii

A Tribute to a Contemporary Mentor
—Master Chin Kung.. xv

Chapter 1: Historical Records of Reincarnation 1
   A Compassionate Order 1
   Cases of Reincarnation Recorded
      Throughout History 2
   The Grievance Between Science and Religion 5

Chapter 2: Modern Scientific Studies on Reincarnation 6
   Over Forty Years of Effort
      to Confirm 3,000 Cases 6
   The Galileo of the Twentieth Century
      —Prof. Ian Stevenson... 10

Chapter 3: Five Areas of Reincarnation Studies.............. 12

Area 1: Study of the Existence of the Soul 13
   Near-Death Experience Studies 13
   Experiments of the Souls' Existence
      and Astral Projection 19
   True Stories That Indicate the Soul's Existence 20
   Quantum Physics Proves the Existence of the Soul 25

Area 2: Study of People Who Remember Their Former Lives **26**

A Fascinating Case Designated by Gandhi 27

A Living Soul in a Dead Body 33

A Thai Monk Reincarnated from His Own Uncle 36

The Former Life of
   Confucian Master Wang Yangming 42

Where Reincarnation and Biology Intersect 46

A Parrot Recalls His Prior Life
   as His Owner's Husband 55

Area 3: Reincarnation Studies Using Hypnosis **56**

Hydrophobia Due to Drowning in a Previous Life 57

The Protagonist of *Many Lives, Many Masters* 62

Alan Lee, an Egyptian Pharaoh in a Former Life 88

Sylvester Stallone Recalls Five Past Lives 90

The Dolphin Who Became a Human 91

Area 4: Studies of Life in Different Dimensions **93**

Talking with Spirits by Radio - proof via sound 94

A Ghastly Surprise in a Graveyard - proof via image 99

Area 5: The Study of Supernatural Power **102**

The Cases of Miracle Worker Cayce 102

Chapter 4: Revealing the Origins of Reincarnation—
   avarice, resentment, attachment, and more **110**

Depression from a Life During World War II 111

A Fear of Birds: A Tragic Retribution for Rape 113

Revenge of the Unfilial Hippies
   and Its Solution 116

Gruesome Response and Retribution
    of a Mother and Child 120
Remembering Being Speared to Death
    by One's Great Uncle 121
Reincarnated as Husband and Sister's Daughter 123

Chapter 5: How to Transcend Reincarnation 125
Natural and Spiritual, in One Meaningful Unity
    —Einstein..126
Manifested by the Heart..127
Manifested in a "Ksana" 129
The Return of Self-Nature 130
Transcend Reincarnation
    with The Pure Land Method 131

Additional Remarks — The Law of Causality................. 137

Afternote — The Method of Reciting Amitabha.............. 157

PREFACE

Many people, after experiencing the genuine benefits of Buddhist teachings, such as inner peace, deeper spiritual enlightenment, and beyond, have asked: "Since Buddhism is phenomenally beneficial, why did Shakyamuni manifest as a Buddha in India to benefit Indian people instead of appearing in other areas like Europe, America, China, or Australia?"

You may ask, "Who was Shakyamuni Buddha?"

Shakyamuni is Sanskrit for "Sage of the Shakya."

Siddhartha Gautama, a royal prince of the Shakya Clan, was born in the sixth century BC in India, near modern Nepal. He is now called Shakyamuni Buddha after becoming enlightened. He became a philosopher and spiritual leader whose teachings are now known as Buddhism. Buddhism, which is considered a spiritual education rather than a religion, focuses on ethical practices, mindfulness, and meditation. The Buddhist world view includes reincarnation—being reborn in subsequent lifetimes—as a path toward ultimate enlightenment.

Now, let's go back to the question; why did Shakyamuni Buddha incarnate in India instead of other regions? The contemporary mentor of the Pure Land School of Buddhism, Master Chin Kung, has unveiled the answer for us. In ancient

India, there were ninety-six religions, and meditation was a prevailing practice among them. Many of the practitioners, through deep meditation, could see different worlds and different dimensions. From the highest dimension of the "heaven of neither perception nor non-perception" (In Sanskrit, devā naivasaṃjñā-nāsaṃjñâyatanôpagāḥ) to the lowest dimension of "avīci hell" (Skt., the hell of incessant suffering), they saw all of the six realms*. Many of them asked:

> *Why are there six realms of reincarnation?*
> *Why is there so much suffering in them?*
> *Are there any other worlds beyond these six realms?*
> *Can we transcend the suffering of these six realms?*

Well, when there is an entreaty, there will be a response. Shakyamuni therefore manifested as a Buddha in India to help them understand the *truth* of life and the universe. Since most of the practitioners had seen the six realms during their deep meditation, they easily accepted His teachings.

Let's think about it this way: Would people in Europe, America, or China who had not practiced meditation and had not seen the six realms believe His teachings? Of course not! That's why it makes perfect sense that Shakyamuni Buddha manifested in India.

---

*Six realms (or six paths) are the realms between birth and death, including the realms of hell, hungry ghost, animal, human, asura, and heaven. They are decided by the state of one's mind.

It is extremely difficult to see all six realms through meditation, yet understanding reincarnation is the key for us to transcend the suffering sea of samsara. Samsara is a Sanskrit word that means "world." It is also the concept of the cycle of death and rebirth, a fundamental belief of most Indian religions. Without understanding and believing in this fact, we will submerge ourselves in

> *The wheel of being deluded,*
> *making karma, and then*
> *receiving retribution (suffering).*

Luckily, modern science has been studying reincarnation since the mid-twentieth century. We owe gratitude to Dr. Zhong Maosen, who spent almost a decade's worth of effort collecting many scientific studies in this area. Not only did he compile these scientific studies into an informative report—which saves a great deal of time for people who are interested in learning—but he even offered a method of transcending this suffering sea of endless birth and death. His contribution is phenomenal!

For more information on related subjects, please visit
http://mahayanapureland.org

ABOUT DR. ZHONG MAOSEN (VENERABLE DING HONG)

Dr. Zhong Maosen was born in Guangzhou, China in 1973. He graduated from Guangzhou Sun Yat-Sen University in 1995 with a bachelor's degree in economics. In 1997, he received an MBA from Louisiana Tech University in the United States, and in 1999 he received a PhD in finance from the same school. He taught at the University of Texas and then Kansas State University for several years.

In 2003, in order to better learn from Master Chin Kung, he moved to Australia and taught at the University of Queensland Business School as an associate professor and doctoral supervisor. During this tenure, he was offered lifetime employment by the university.

As an admirer of the eminent monk Master Chin Kung's great virtue and teachings, Dr. Zhong Maosen has followed and learned from him since his college years. In 2006, Dr. Zhong Maosen renounced the worldly pursuit of being a professor and started to learn preaching on classics of Chinese culture under Master Chin Kung's guidance. He also served as an English interpreter for Master Chin Kung at international peace and education activities.

In July 2011, Dr. Zhong Maosen was ordained with the dharma-name "Ding Hong" under the seat of Venerable Master Chang Huai in Hong Kong. He later dedicated himself to propagating *The Infinite Life Sutra* and vowing to fulfill

> *The lifelong effort of Master Chin Kung—*
> *to restore the function of Buddhism as "education."*

In 2013, Venerable Ding Hong was sent by Master Chin Kung to learn Buddhist precepts from Master Preceptor (Skt. Vinaya-Dhara) Guo Qing in Taiwan. After completing several years of learning the precepts, he continued teaching the precepts and Buddha Dharma throughout Chinese communities.

His speeches on the topics of causal education, revelations of new discoveries in space physics, Chinese traditional culture, scientifically validated Buddhism, and *The Infinite Life Sutra* have been well-received by the general public.

A TRIBUTE TO A CONTEMPORARY MENTOR—MASTER CHIN KUNG

In order to pay tribute to the contemporary mentor of Pure Land Buddhism, Master Chin Kung, for his tireless teaching over half a century to bring a light to the darkness of our samsara and lead us to an enlightening path, the Mahayana Pure Land Team translated his speech on *The Law of Causality*.

It is included here along with the translation on the lecture of *The Scientific Proof of Causal Reincarnation* by his protégé, Venerable Ding Hong (formerly known as Dr. Zhong Maosen). We hope to spread the *truth* of life and the universe through these remarkable teachings, dedicating the merits to the awakening of all sentient beings and world peace.

Please allow us to introduce to you this extraordinary contemporary mentor.

Venerable Master Chin Kung, born 1927 in Lujiang, Anhui, China, is an eminent monk in the Pure Land school of Mahayana Buddhism. He is an advisor to more than 100 Amitabha Buddhist Societies and Pure Land Learning Centers worldwide.

Master Chin Kung pioneered the use of the Internet and satellite television in promulgating the Buddha's teachings. His recorded lectures have been distributed freely in print, as well as on DVDs, CDs, and other media worldwide.

His study of Buddhism began from his twenties, learning philosophy from a great philosopher, Professor Thomé H. Fang (Fang Dongmei), who told him,

> *"Shakyamuni Buddha was*
> *the world's greatest philosopher.*
> *Buddhist philosophy is*
> *the summit of world philosophy.*
> *And learning Buddhism is*
> *the greatest enjoyment of life."*

Fascinated by this statement, he was drawn to delve deeper. Later he started formally learning from Master Zhangjia (Janggya Hotogtu), a renowned Mongolian monk of the Tibetan Buddhist tradition who imparted him the key of obtaining the genuine benefits of Buddhism:

> *"See through to the truth and*
> *let go of all worldly attachments."*

After diligently practicing for several years, he brought forth the aspiration to spread the Buddha's teaching and followed Mr. Li Bingnan, a lay practitioner and a Master in both Buddhism and Confucianism, to learn the traditional method of preaching Buddhist sutras.

Master Chin Kung is a mentor in Pure Land Buddhism who spared no effort to promote world peace. Having successfully united nine major religions in Singapore, he has been invited to UNESCO conferences since 2006. Following his success in Singapore, Master Chin Kung focused his effort on helping other countries, such as Australia and Indonesia, to advance their religious solidarity.

The UNESCO ambassadors were deeply inspired and encouraged by his philosophy after visiting and witnessing the exemplary cities that were transformed according to his teachings. In July 2017, they hence founded the "Association of Master Chin Kung's Friends at UNESCO" with the goal of facilitating religious solidarity in more countries, and ultimately, helping achieve world peace.

The major part of this book, *The Scientific Proof of Causal Reincarnation*, is drawn from a lecture given in the early part of the Chinese New Year in 2006 by Dr. Zhong Maosen, who admired Master Chin Kung's great virtue and followed his teachings throughout his life.

CHAPTER ONE

HISTORICAL RECORDS OF REINCARNATION

Distinguished nobles, venerables, and practitioners, Happy New Year, everyone!

I am very grateful that President Wu gave me such an introduction. I do not deserve it. I feel very honored to be able to visit this "treasure island" (Formosa/Taiwan) today. This is the first time I have stepped foot on this island. And this is my first speech—*The Scientific Proof of Causal Reincarnation*—right here in Liuhe Pure Land Society. It shows that we have a deep affinity. So I am very grateful to all of you for making time today to come and listen to my report on the topic of causal reincarnation. It is indeed a very important sage education.

A COMPASSIONATE ORDER

I just returned from Hong Kong. In Hong Kong, I gave our mentor, Master Chin Kung, New Year's greetings and celebrated his eightieth birthday. He told me that causality education is the most important education to save the world.

In the past, Great Master Yin Guang emphasized causality education above even Buddhist scriptures. So Master Chin Kung gave me a compassionate order: to travel around the world, using the scientific perspective to report facts of causal reincarnation to all. Thus, I greatly appreciate you all for coming here to support me.

Over the past years, I have been compiling and studying scientific research from Western scientists, scholars, and professors in the area of causal reincarnation. I have reviewed a great number of cases. I summarized and concluded these cases in order to give this report. It is also a report of my personal learning experience. I cordially hope that you can kindly give me critiques and corrections.

CASES OF REINCARNATION
RECORDED THROUGHOUT HISTORY

Humans are born, and thus they must die. Ever since humans have known of birth and death, they have started to explore some more profound issues. For example,

Why do people experience birth and death?
Can we escape from birth and death?

These questions actually have been explored for thousands of years throughout human history. Many religious and traditional cultures offer an abundance of answers. For example, more than two thousand years ago, the Chinese sage Confucius had an annotation in *The Book of Changes (I Ching)*:

Refined energy turns into matter, and
a drifting soul is changed by conditions.

"Refined energy turns into matter" refers to the situation after birth, while the drifting soul indicates the condition before birth.

Throughout his lifelong teaching, Confucius never accentuated his teaching on death but encouraged us to focus on current life cultivation. He said, "Without knowing birth, how can one know death?" However, in his annotation above, he had essentially revealed to us the truth of birth and death.

In the same era as Confucius, there was a Western sage, Plato. Among his works, there is one book titled *The Republic* where he also mentioned the experiences of a soul leaving a body. In addition, the sage of Buddhism, Shakyamuni Buddha, gave very detailed explanations about the six realms of reincarnation as well.

In fact, there is a lot of recorded information regarding birth and death—reincarnation—within both Eastern and Western history, including quite a few examples in the official history. Let me cite some examples as our introduction here. These are recorded in Chinese "official history," which means these stories are recognized by the nation.

Of Poets, Emperors, and Monks

A poet in the Tang Dynasty, Li Bai—also known as the "Immortal Poet"—was reincarnated in the Song Dynasty as Guo Xiangzheng. This is recorded in the 10th post, 3rd volume, 444th chapter of *The History of the Song Dynasty*.

The former life of Emperor Yuan of Liang, in the Southern and Northern Dynasties, was as a monk named Miaomu Seng. Observing from history, we can see that emperors and people with great fortune and power were usually practitioners in the past. This record is an excerpt from the 1st post, 3rd volume, 8th chapter, in *Liang's Annals of Southern History*.

The record also includes instances of the reincarnation of heavenly beings. For instance, in the history of the Tang Dynasty, Emperor Daizong was reincarnated from a deity. This is recorded in the 3rd post, 7th volume, 27th chapter, in *The Book of Tang*.

Struck by Lightning
Life after Life as an Animal

Of course, animals are also mentioned; that is, people have reincarnated as animals. The most famous example is from the Spring-Autumn and Warring States periods. A general of the Qin state, Bai Qi, led his army to fight against the Zhao state.

General Zhao Kuo of the Zhao state only understood military tactics on paper and didn't understand how to use military force, so he lost. As a result, four hundred thousand soldiers of the Zhao Army were captured by the Qin general Bai Qi, and Bai Qi had the four hundred thousand prisoners buried alive. In doing so, he committed a deep sin. This history was recorded in a famous history book, *The Chronicles of the Eastern Zhou Kingdoms*. Its original words were this:

> *At the end of the Tang Dynasty,*
> *an ox was struck dead by lightning.*
> *On the belly of this ox was written the words "Bai Qi."*

The critics said that Bai Qi had killed too many people, therefore he received the retribution of being reborn as an animal and struck by lightning for hundreds of years. According to the legend, many people, when slaughtering pigs, saw the words "Bai Qi" after the pig hair was removed. This implies that Bai Qi was reincarnated life after life to receive his retribution.

We can only mention a few of the many records in ancient history because our focus today is on scientific cases. Due to so many records in "official history," the ancients had no doubts at all about the truth of causal reincarnation.

THE GRIEVANCE
BETWEEN SCIENCE AND RELIGION

Today, science has progressed, and people have begun to believe in science with blind faith. Many think that science offers facts and evidence, so they no longer believe in causal reincarnation. They consider reincarnation a religious concept. Some use science to criticize religion and claim that reincarnation in religion is anti-science. Why would this be?

It's likely because science and religion have had grievances for hundreds of years. In the 17th century, Italian astronomer Galileo Galilei proposed that the Earth was not the center of the universe. At that time, the religious believers, who were Catholics, embraced the idea that the Earth was the center of the universe and had been created by God. As a result, Galileo was persecuted by the clergy. They rebuked his scientific discoveries as heresy and imprisoned him for life. Many scientists were also persecuted at the time, including Italian monk and philosopher Giordano Bruno, who was burned at the stake.

The grievances between science and religion have caused people to use science to discredit religion today. In the past, people used religion against science. This is called "an eye for an eye" or causal retribution.

CHAPTER TWO

MODERN SCIENTIFIC STUDIES ON REINCARNATION

Science has many ways to test the truth. In recent decades, Western science has made great progress in developing the scientific areas in psychiatry, death, physiology, and psychology. Scientific scholars have confirmed that people indeed experience reincarnation.

OVER FORTY YEARS OF EFFORT TO CONFIRM 3,000 CASES

Let's introduce these scientific achievements. The first case is from the University of Virginia, by a professor of psychiatry named Ian Stevenson. The main subjects of this professor's study were children between two and seven years of age. These children—who came from all over the world, including the United States, Canada, South America, Europe, West Asia, and Southeast Asia—could all remember details from their previous lives.

Stevenson took more than forty years to compile his study of some 3,000 confirmed cases of reincarnation. The children in those case studies, though very young, were able to accurately state events from the past few decades or even from past centuries. They were able to describe these things in great detail.

While I was teaching in American universities, I contacted Professor Stevenson. At the time, he had published several books, including *Twenty Cases Suggestive of Reincarnation*, which is the masterpiece of his work.

A Four-Year-Old Invited Her Dad
to Her Past Life's House

I would like to report another case to you. It is about a girl in India named Swarnlata who could remember the circumstances of her past life. She was born on March 2, 1948 and lived with her family in an Indian city called Pradesh.

When Swarnlata was four years old, she could describe some experiences of her own former life. She said that in her past life she lived in another city in India called Katni. Her family name was Pathak, and she had a husband and children. The families of her past life and this life were total strangers to each other and geographically far apart. One day, her father took her past the city where she had lived in her past life.

Suddenly, she said to her father, "Daddy, daddy, my house is near here! Let's go visit and have some tea." Her father said, "You silly child! Our house is still far away from here."

But after that, her father often heard his young daughter talk about her encounters from her past life. Later, when this case became known to Dr. Stevenson and some of his colleagues in India, they began to carry out investigations. With Swarnlata's guidance, the researchers found the family of her past life.

In the process, this little girl Swarnlata's past life was revealed: She had been named Biya and she died in 1939, leaving her husband and two sons behind.

Meeting the Family of Her Past Life

When these professors took this little girl to the family of her past life, she was able to name each family member with perfect precision. At that time, the professors conducted a test: In order to observe her accuracy, the investigators deliberately tried to mislead her by introducing one of her former children as someone else instead. Nevertheless, when this little girl saw the son of her past life, she hugged him and said, "This is my son, his name is Murli."

Rather than being affected by the professors' attempt to mislead her, this little girl—despite now being younger than the son of her former life—still could not help but naturally show a mother's love and care for him.

Even more interestingly, this little girl revealed one of her past husband's secrets. How?

As it turns out, one day her husband had gone into her cash box, taking her personal money, 1,200 rupees, and he had never returned the money to her. No one but the husband knew this had happened. At first, he had denied taking the money, but after Swarnlata's visit, he finally admitted that it had indeed happened.

> *This was regarded as evidence*
> *of the existence of reincarnation later.*

You see, if we owe somebody money, even if it is from a past life, the creditor will remember this fact in his heart. So, we should never have unpaid debts, for they cannot be escaped.

Nine Years of Singing and Dancing
in Bangladesh

You might have noticed that this little girl said that in her past life she was a mother named Biya who died in 1939. But in this life, the little girl was born in 1948. Where did she go for the nine years in between? Swarnlata told researchers that she reincarnated and lived in a village in what is now Bangladesh. In that life, the girl had passed away at the age of nine. So the timing matches up perfectly.

But how did they prove this reincarnation?

It turns out that Swarnlata, from a young age, loved to sing and dance to a folk song from Bangladesh. Her family in the present life did not understand Bengali, so her parents never knew what she was singing about. They thought she was lost in her own imagination.

One of the professors investigating Swarnlata understood Bengali. He quickly wrote down the lyrics when Swarnlata was singing. The lyrics, which Professor Stevenson included in his paper, praised nature and described the joy of farmers at their harvest. It was very beautiful. The professors, following this little girl's directions, located the village of her past life in Bangladesh. After some verification, they discovered that the villagers all loved to sing and dance to this same song. It was very popular locally.

Swarnlata was a normal young Indian girl who grew up to earn a bachelor's degree in engineering from an Indian university at age nineteen and a master's degree in engineering at age twenty-one. Two years later, she began to teach at a highly accredited institution in India. She kept in contact with Dr. Stevenson, even after she became an adult. So she is a person with a typical mind.

Swarnlata is a living example of reincarnation. Her memories give us a strong confirmation that reincarnation does exist.

THE GALILEO OF THE TWENTIETH CENTURY —PROF. IAN STEVENSON

Because modern people admire science and require scientific proof, Professor Stevenson used a scientific perspective and attitude to conduct his studies on reincarnation. He was not a religious person. When I contacted him, he said that he did not want to be known as religious or have any connection to religion, it would affect the credibility of his scientific research if he associated himself with religion.

The spirit of science has a few requirements:

1. First is discerning truth by using facts revealed in actual experiments. All of the experiments and cases must lead to the same truth for that truth to be accepted as fact.
2. The results of the scientific experiments must be repeatable. That is to say, Experiment A gets certain results, Experiment B conducted in another country gets the same results, and Experiment C conducted a year later gets the same results as well. The truth is repeatable if various experiments confirm it, regardless of time or location.

With this scientific spirit, as Professor Stevenson researched more than 3,000 cases over forty years, he was scrupulous about every detail. The facts of reincarnation that he confirmed have earned high praise from the scientific community and academia. In *The Journal of Nervous and Mental Disease*, an article stated,

> *Either Dr. Stevenson is making a colossal mistake,*
> *or he will be known as the Galileo of the 20th century.*

We just introduced the original Galileo; he is the Father of Modern Science, a man who dedicated himself to science. Why would a magazine honor Professor Stevenson as the Galileo of the 20th century?

Although Galileo's scientific discoveries are common knowledge today, in his time, they were considered a huge assault on religious ideas. Similarly, the facts of reincarnation that Professor Stevenson discovered and confirmed also stand in stark contrast to the accepted norms of today's thought. More research in the future will certainly confirm these discoveries.

Next, I would like to introduce to you all, little by little, the research by the Western scientific community in the area of reincarnation.

CHAPTER THREE

FIVE AREAS of
REINCARNATION STUDIES

Research by Western scientists in the area of reincarnation has been deep and extensive. I have attempted to classify the studies into five scientific areas. The areas are not necessarily exact, but they should provide a general idea.

1. The study of the existence of the soul.
2. Case studies of people who remember their past lives.
3. The study of using hypnosis.
4. The study of life in different dimensions.
5. The study of people with supernatural abilities.

These five areas use different angles to prove reincarnation.

I have chosen some of the more exciting cases from each area and will discuss the research that was done. We will see that people do experience reincarnation and that the endless birth and death causes much pain and suffering. We will explore some profound questions, such as:

What causes reincarnation?
Are there any ways to transcend reincarnation?

STUDY OF THE EXISTENCE OF THE SOUL

A primary premise of studying reincarnation is to recognize that people do have a soul. If souls do not exist, then what is being reincarnated? So our first topic of discussion is to prove the existence of the soul.

Most cultures, in ancient as well as in modern times, in the east and west, have some concept of the soul. A great number of people have reported actually seeing a soul, whether they call it a "ghost" or "spirit." Perhaps even some of you here have seen them as well. However, without "hard scientific evidence," it is still difficult for many people to accept that the soul exists.

NEAR-DEATH EXPERIENCE STUDIES

In recent decades, Western science has looked for scientific evidence to prove the existence of the soul by studying what is called "Near-Death Experience" (NDE.) The idea is that when a person is "near death" or on the brink of death, this person experiences a different relationship to his or her soul. Some people who are dying have experienced their souls traveling outside of their bodies. For example, a patient who almost dies during surgery might see a variety of scenes that make him feel his soul has left his body. Later, when he has recovered, he will tell others what he experienced. This is called a near-death experience.

According to the well-known American research and polling company Gallup, out-of-body, near-death experiences are common in the United States. At least 13 million adults who are still alive today reported having had a near-death experience. If we include children, the number would be even more impressive.

According to a well-known American scholar from the University of Connecticut, Dr. Kenneth Ring, about 35 percent of people have had near-death experiences. The NDE phenomenon has now attracted scientists from many different fields, including University of Washington professor of Pediatrics Dr. Melvin Morse, University of Nevada Dr. Raymond A. Moody, and University of California professor Dr. Charles Tart. In addition, Dr. Elisabeth Kübler-Ross, the American author and psychiatrist who was an expert on death and dying, also has studied NDEs.

Reports of near-death experiences are often published in famous medical journals such as *The Journal of Near-Death Studies* and *The Lancet*. In 1978, at the initiative of some authoritative scholars, The International Association for Near-Death Studies (IANDS) was formally established. We could say that the research in this area is just unfolding.

Typical Near-Death Experiences

As a matter of fact, the study of NDEs began as early as 1959. American parapsychologist Dr. Karlis Osis, after investigating hundreds of cases of patients' deaths, co-authored a book titled *At the Hour of Death* in which he summarized the more common characteristics of near-death experiences.

Dr. Osis wrote that many patients nearing death felt confusion and memory loss, but a small number were able to maintain a lucid mind until the last minute. These clear-minded people claimed that they saw their afterlife. Some reported seeing the spirits of deceased family and friends, religious and mythical characters, or a spiritual light and a beautiful otherworldly environment. They described these experiences as emotionally powerful, bringing them peace, tranquility, and religious affinity.

Between 1972 and 1974, Dr. Raymond Moody from the University of Nevada conducted a similar study of 150 near-death cases. His book about this study, called *Life After Life*, became well-known. Moody's study confirmed much of Dr. Osis' research. Moody concluded:

> *When a person was dying, lying on the surgery table, his physical body felt excruciating pain. He would hear the doctor's announcements: "This person has died." He would hear some noise, some ringing or buzzing, and then he would feel like he was quickly passing through a black tunnel.*
>
> *Afterward, he would feel like he had left his body and would see his body lying on the surgery table from a distance. He began to feel very strange but slowly adapted to this strange sensation. He would find that, in addition to the body he just departed, he had another body. But this body was not in the form of a physical body, it was a soul in the form of light.*

Gods and Spirits of the Great Beyond

Some of Moody's research subjects saw visions, such as some of the spirits of their deceased relatives and friends.

Some reported seeing gods who were familiar and welcoming. For example, Christians would see Jesus; of course, we know that people who recite Amitabha* would see Amitabha. They described these beings as manifesting in the form of a flashing light.

The cases Moody studied were all Westerners, and mostly of the Christian faith. They described a luminous form of life, a god, who used a nonverbal method to communicate with them. They discovered there was no need to use language to communicate! The god let them evaluate their own lives and then rapidly showed them the major incidents of their lives, as if they were watching a movie. After they finished watching, these people would still feel an affinity with our world, so they would wake up again.

Sometimes we do things that many people do not know, or even that nobody knows. But according to the NDE research subjects, when the soul has left the body because death is near, various "gods" would show us all of

---

*Amitabha is the Buddha of The Pure Land of Ultimate Bliss where there is no suffering but all joys. This land is also known as Sukhāvatī in Sanskrit. Buddhism teaches that there are countless Buddhas in the universe and that anyone can attain Buddhahood. By attaining Buddhahood, people can escape the six realms of endless reincarnation: heaven, asura, human, animal, ghost, and hell. Amitabha is acclaimed as "The King of All Buddhas." People recite His name, Amitabha, in order to be reborn into The Pure Land of Ultimate Bliss, where they can quickly attain Buddhahood in one lifetime due to more favorable cultivation conditions. The difference between Sukhavati and the heavens is that those reborn in Sukhavati are forever beyond birth and death.

the good and bad things we have done. Chinese ancestors often said:

What is done by night appears by day.

The following Daoist (Taoist) sayings are indeed very insightful:

Three feet above our heads there are gods;
the good and evil karmas we have committed
are all under the watch and on the records of gods.

Many of the people studied describe their experiences thusly: Before they came back, they felt like they were about to cross some kind of boundary, the boundary separating this life from the afterlife. But they did not cross over; they returned to Earth instead. Some said that they did not want to return to the Earth. Why? Because human life has too much suffering. Yet they felt they had to come back to the body on the surgery table even though they wanted to linger in that spiritual life. They felt an invisible force pulling them back, so they had no choice but to return to their physical body.

A Terrifying Near-Death Experience

Of course, not all of the near-death experiences studied were wonderful reunions with a spiritual light. Some were terrifying. In *Impressions of Heaven*, a book of stories taken from the oral statements of 100 survivors, a German police chief named Stein Heidler reported a terrible near-death experience. In his life, Heidler had been cruel and indifferent to people.

With no loving heart and a strong brusqueness, he must have treated prisoners very harshly.

When Heidler was near death, he found himself surrounded by fearsome ghosts baring their fangs and brandishing their claws. One of the ghosts even opened his big, bloody mouth and tried to bite him. Heidler found his near-death experience horrific.

Buddhist scriptures also have included near-death experiences. Around three thousand years ago, the Buddha described near-death experiences in detail. One example is in *The Sutra of Bodhisattva Kṣitigarbha's Fundamental Vows*, which contains this paragraph:

> *The sentient beings of Jambudvipa*
> *(referring to our Earth),*
> *even those who have done good deeds,*
> *at the end of their life,*
> *will have hundreds of thousands of evil spirits*
> *in the forms of their parents or relatives*
> *to tempt them to the evil paths.*
> *Can you imagine what would happen*
> *to those who have done evil deeds?*

This means that people of our world, even kind-hearted ones, as they approach death will inevitably encounter spirits of the evil paths, such as hungry ghosts, to make them suffer. These evil spirits might disguise themselves in the forms of the family members to confuse and entice them to the evil paths. Or they might appear as monsters, as they did to German police officer Heidler.

Psychologist Dr. Elisabeth Kübler-Ross has written two masterpieces: one is *On Life After Death* and the other is *On Death and Dying*. During her lifetime, she researched more than 20,000 cases and confirmed that there are a variety of near-death experiences, as reported by people who came back after their souls had left their bodies. The works of Dr. Kübler-Ross have been translated into many languages and are popular around the world.

EXPERIMENTS OF THE SOUL'S EXISTENCE AND ASTRAL PROJECTION

The first person to use scientific experiments to confirm that the soul exists was a British doctor named Dr. Sam Parnia. He designed an experiment specifically for patients at their time of death. He hung a piece of wood from the ceiling above the surgery table and put some objects on the wood. Only the doctor knew what these small objects were. The patients did not know. He then conducted a test on more than 100 patients who had almost died but had been revived on the surgery table. Many of these patients were able to accurately describe what they saw on the wood at the time their souls had left their bodies and drifted to the top of the room.

Although his experiment was simple—the soul seeing a designated object after leaving the body and coming back to tell him—Dr. Parnia indeed confirmed that the existence of people's souls is an objective existence. The phenomenon of the soul leaving the body is common in people who are about to die, but people who are alive may also experience this phenomenon. Many people possess the ability to voluntarily separate their souls from their bodies in a process called "astral projection."

At the University of California, Professor Charles Tart conducted scientific experiments on healthy people who claimed their souls had left their bodies. He used a computer to print out a randomly generated, five-digit number. He then put this paper on a high shelf and began to ask his subjects if they were able to see the number while "out of body."

One young woman who volunteered for this experiment claimed she had the ability of astral projection. She was told to lie down and separate her soul from her body. They instructed her, "After your soul has left your body, float to the top of the room, memorize the number on the piece of paper, and then come back to tell us." After a few minutes, she came back and precisely told them the number on the paper.

According to mathematical probability, the odds of correctly guessing a randomly generated five-digit number is one in 100,000. That means that, in one hundred thousand attempts, you might only guess it correctly once. Yet this woman was tested several times and answered correctly every time.

The experiment proved that she did not guess—she really saw it.

This professor used the scientific method to prove that humans have a soul and that the soul can see and even memorize information. To do these things, the soul must have some kind of energy of its own when it is separated from the body.

With this energy, the soul can do very significant work.

TRUE STORIES THAT INDICATE THE SOUL'S EXISTENCE

Let me tell you two true stories first, from a book titled *Mysteries of the Inner Self*, published in 1992 by Straut Holroyd of England. The first story, "The Soul That Rescued a Ship in Distress," is a classic that has been well-researched by the scientific community. It was originally published in 1860 in Robert Owen's book, *Walk on the Edge of the Spiritual World*.

Story One:
A Soul That Rescued a Ship in Distress

In 1828, the first mate of a merchant ship that traveled between England and Canada entered his captain's office. The ship had been at sea for six weeks, and the captain was watching the weather from the deck.

In the captain's office, the first mate, whose name was Bruce, discovered a man he had never seen before writing something on a note board. When the man looked up at him, stony-faced, it gave him goosebumps! Bruce ran to tell the captain that someone he didn't recognize, with an unsettling facial expression, was in his office. They quickly returned to the office—but nobody was there. The note board was still there, bearing the words: *Sail to the northwest.*

The captain asked, "Are you trying to trick me, Bruce? Or deliberately making up some story?"

The first mate said, "I swear, I just saw this person writing these exact words."

The captain asked the first mate to also write the words, *Sail to the northwest.*

The handwriting was completely different. Then the captain had all of the crew write these words, but none of their handwriting matched. The captain was puzzled. They had been at sea for six weeks! How could a complete stranger appear on the ship? They searched from bow to stern, but they could not find him on the ship.

The wind was calm at the time. Although it would be a detour of a few hours to head northwest, the captain gave the order to obey the mysterious note. The ship set off. About three hours later, they saw an iceberg ahead. A ship had struck the iceberg and was stuck in the ice.

People onboard were frantically waving to them for help. The captain immediately ordered the lifeboat deployed, and his crew rescued the stranded people, one by one. Among those who were rescued, First Mate Bruce saw someone he recognized. It was the stranger whom he had seen in the captain's office.

He excitedly pointed the man out to the captain, who called him over and asked him to write these few words: *Sail to the northwest.* The handwriting was exactly the same. Even the man himself could not explain it. "Huh? How did my writing get onto that note board?"

Everyone came to ask him, "What's going on?"

Slowly, the memory came back to him.

"About three hours ago, after our boat got stuck, everybody was rushing to help. We were all very tired. So I laid down on the bed and fell asleep."

He said that he had a dream about a boat that would rescue them. After he woke up, he told his shipmates not to worry, because help was on the way. He even described the appearance, the color, and the shape of the boat he had seen in his dream. Others from the ship confirmed what he said. The man had told them about his dream a few hours earlier. And the ship that came to their rescue was the ship he described.

It appears that the soul of this unknown man left his body while he was sleeping aboard the distressed ship. His soul then found a ship to rescue them, and he was even able to leave his writing on the note board: *Sail to the northwest.*

The note board is "hard scientific evidence" that the soul can leave the body. The soul has enough energy not only to travel, but to leave a note! The soul is not limited by our three or four dimensions. Three dimensions refer to space: length, width, and height. Time is the fourth dimension. The soul was not bound by time and space, so it could quickly reach any place he wanted to go.

Our soul can transcend!
Our soul goes beyond time and space!

Time and Space
Are an Illusion of Mankind

In fact, modern physics has confirmed that time and space themselves are illusions of mankind. These are the words of the Father of Modern Physics, Albert Einstein. He said, "Time and space are an illusion of mankind."

Why? Because his Theory of Relativity confirmed that both time and space are determined by the relative speed of an object. When an object is moving at high speeds, the time of this object will be lengthened, a phenomenon called "time dilation." At the same time, the object's length will be shortened and its space shrunk. This has been proven by modern physics theories. Time and space are variable factors; they are not absolute or concrete. That is why Einstein called them an illusion.

The Buddha also told us that time and space are human delusions. You see, the "illusion" and "delusion" are equally matched!

After the soul leaves the body, it can go beyond some limitations of time and space. It can drift quickly through space. Confucius called such a soul "a drifting soul"!

Story Two:
A Soul That Bought a House

A woman in Ireland often had astral projection experiences. One time, while she was astral projecting, she saw a house that she was fond of. Afterward, her soul visited this house several times. She really liked the house, from the inside to the outside, from the furniture to the layout. She liked it all. But she did not know where this house was.

Later, she and her husband moved from Ireland to London. They searched the advertisements for a bargain house and visited a few. The woman immediately recognized the house she had seen in her astral projections. From the inside to the outside as well as the layout, the decoration, the color, everything was exactly the same as what she saw. And the price was surprisingly cheap! The agent warned them that the house was haunted, but they decided to buy it anyway. So, they made an appointment to meet with the owner. As soon as they saw each other, the owner screamed out loud, "Ah! It is you, the ghost!"

The owner had seen this woman many times in his house. What he saw was her spirit, but he thought his house was haunted and wanted to sell it as quickly as possible.

A Free Spirit Becomes
a Slave to the Body

Ireland and London are more than 400 kilometers apart. The soul can indeed go beyond the distance of more than 400 kilometers; it can travel freely, without obstacles. As we can see, the soul is not constrained by time and space like our physical body is. But in reality,

Isn't our body just like the house of our soul?
Isn't reincarnation just like our soul looking for a new house?

If we become attached to this body and think of it as ourselves, then we are constrained by this physical house. In order to satisfy our physical desires, we also create innumerable karmas by killing, stealing, lying, sexual misconduct, etc. Our attempts to satisfy our desires lead to greed, resentment, ignorance, and arrogance.

The soul should be the master of our physical body—but if we become attached to the body, our soul becomes its slave. We then do many shameful deeds to satisfy our bodies. The ancient Chinese philosopher Laozi* once said,

My biggest worry is that I have this body.

QUANTUM PHYSICS
PROVES THE EXISTENCE OF THE SOUL

A group of physicists using modern physics, especially quantum mechanics, argue that the existence of the soul is indeed objective in theory.

One of these physicists is a well-known Indian-American professor and world-famous researcher at the Institute of Noetic Sciences, Dr. Amit Goswami. He used quantum mechanics to

---

*Laozi was an ancient Chinese philosopher and writer. He is the reputed author of the *Tao Te Ching* and the founder of philosophical Taoism.

argue that humans have a soul. So in reality, not only have scientists confirmed the existence of the soul through the scientific method, but they have also explained it in theory. Dr. Goswami described his conclusion in a book called *Physics for the Soul*. Another scientist has been to our Queensland University to speak on this topic. He is also an American professor using physics to argue for the existence of the soul.

This is my simple report regarding modern scientific research in the first area: the existence of the soul. It proves that people have a soul and this soul has energy. The soul can see, hear, and memorize, it can even buy a house! And this soul, of course, after leaving the body, will go somewhere else. This process is called "reincarnation."

AREA TWO :

STUDY OF PEOPLE WHO REMEMBER THEIR FORMER LIVES

The second area of scientific research into reincarnation involves case studies of people who claim to remember their former lives. Professor Stevenson of the University of Virginia and his colleagues used a traditional approach, which includes the following:

1. Discover the object
2. Obtain information
3. Collect the information
4. Make a case
5. Obtain evidence
6. Track observations
7. Write a report

The characteristics of this method are logical and objective, and its evidence is both credible and persuasive. The problem is that the time, manpower, and budget needed are often too large. For example, from making a case to the last step of confirming the evidence to write a report usually takes several years; it can even take more than a decade. So it is not easy to do this type of research.

A FASCINATING CASE
DESIGNATED BY GANDHI

One famous case is a classic example in the study of reincarnation from the 1930s. It involves an Indian girl, Shanti Devi. Her case is unusual because it was investigated by members of a committee designated by Mahatma Gandhi, the Father of India.

Indian scholar Dr. K.S. Rawat—who, like Professor Stevenson, devoted his life to the study of reincarnation—made the report. Later, this case was published in March 1997 in *Venture Inward Magazine,* a publication of the late psychic Edgar Cayce's Association for Research and Enlightenment.

Shanti was born in the city of Delhi, India. Early in life, she claimed she could remember her previous life. She said that she had lived in the Indian city of Mathura. She was married to a man named Pandit Kedar Nath Chaube, the owner of the first small cloth shop in that area. Her past life name had been Lugdi. Lugdi suffered complications during childbirth in 1925. She delivered a son by C-section but died nine days later. One year and ten months after her death—on December 11, 1926—she was born again in Delhi.

How Could Little Shanti
Know So Much About C-Sections?

Shanti began describing the details of her past life as soon as she was able to talk, including the fact that she died from the C-section. At the time, her parents both thought that their daughter was talking nonsense. But one day, a doctor friend who came to visit the family heard this little six-year-old girl describing the process of a C-section in great detail. He was shocked. Why? Because even he was not as familiar with the complex C-section surgery as this little girl.

Shanti Meets
Her Previous Family

After this incident, the parents began to give more credence to Shanti's stories. The little girl even remembered her previous address. Her parents wrote to the family at that address and invited them to meet. When the professors heard about this case, they also came to investigate and recorded the process and their findings.

These two families did not know each other, but after receiving the letter, Shanti's past-life husband, Kedar Nath, confirmed that Shanti's description of her past life was mostly true. He agreed to visit this little girl and brought along his brother, his second wife, and his son. This son was the one she gave birth to by C-section.

Still Remembers the Favorite Food
of Her Past Husband

At that time, the scholars began to do some tests. They pointed to her husband's brother deliberately to confuse her and said, "This is Kedar Nath, your husband in your past life." But the little girl said, "No, no, he is not my husband, my husband should be him!" She pointed to the one who was really her husband and told her parents, "Didn't I tell you? I said my husband has a mole on his nose and wears glasses. His skin is very light. It is him!"

She was not confused by the deceptions at all.

When these two families met, Shanti's mother invited the guests for lunch. The little girl told everyone her husband's favorite foods as if describing family valuables. She said her husband liked to eat potato pancakes and liked to drink pumpkin juice. When Kedar Nath heard this, he was startled. How could this little girl know him so clearly? Later, he spent some time alone with this little girl and said to the professor afterward, "I believe, without a doubt, that this little girl's past life was indeed as my wife." This was because they talked about a lot of details of their married life which were impossible for anybody else to have known.

No Obstacle Between Hearts

When little Shanti saw the son she had given birth to by C-section, she burst into tears. This is a mother's deep affection for her son, even though he was now older than her. She quickly ran to her room and brought out all of her toys to offer to her son.

People asked, "At the death of your past life, your son was just a newborn baby. How could you even know that he is your son?" Shanti answered, "My son is part of my heart. Even if the body is different, there is no obstacle between hearts." Everyone was surprised that this little girl could say such words!

As we know, the relationship of familial love between parents and children is inherent, so our ancestors said,

> *Beloved affection between parents and children*
> *is pure nature and purely innate.*

Shanti's love for her son, even in a different life, had no obstacle. The ancient Chinese sages taught us about morals and ethics. They said this of the Five Ethical Relationships:

> *There is inborn love*
> *between parents and children, and*
> *there must be righteousness*
> *between leaders and subordinates.*
> *There are distinct responsibilities*
> *between husband and wife, and*
> *there must be a proper order*
> *between the young and the old.*
> *And lastly, there should be trustworthiness*
> *among friends.*

Of all these, the core truth is "There is inborn love between parents and children." This means the innate affection between parents and children is natural. It is not taught by others. Only if we follow the nature of this beloved affection between parents and children to educate the public, can the hearts of human beings be saved and society return to order.

In Confucianism, filial piety is the virtue of demonstrating respect for one's parents, elders, and ancestors. Society has become chaotic because of the lack of filial piety nowadays!

Only a Pure, Loving Heart Is Eternal

When little Shanti was speaking with her former life's husband, she described enough details of their lives to convince him of her identity. Shanti pointed at his second wife and said,

"Didn't we make an agreement that you would never remarry?" This made her husband very embarrassed.

You see, the kind of love that our worldly people speak about—romance—is like popular songs describe: My love for you will be everlasting until the seas dry up and the rocks crumble. Yet this kind of love cannot be relied upon, because

A vow stimulated out of the desire for love is not reliable.
Only the kind of love arising from a pure heart will be eternal.
Like the vow of Buddhas and Bodhisattvas
arising from their compassion—love from a pure heart—
will be true and eternal.

Burst Out Sobbing
When Seeing Her Past Parents

The story of little Shanti's tale spread throughout India and throughout the world. The Father of India, Mahatma Gandhi, organized a committee of fifteen experts to investigate her case.

On November 24, 1935, the committee took little Shanti to find the home of her past life's husband. On this visit, little Shanti was like a tour guide, describing what would be ahead and even what route to take. She seemed to be familiar with this area, although she had never been here in this life; it was all from the memory of her past life. When these people arrived at her former husband's house, she recognized her father-in-law at first glance.

Next, she returned to her own parents' house, which was nearby. Her parents were elderly and had silver hair. When little Shanti saw them, she hugged her parents and burst out sobbing.

The experts at the scene, the members of the committee, were very touched. So you see, in her former life, she died before her parents! A single breath not taken will send one to the next life!

One Missed Breath
Sends You to the Next Life

One day, when the Buddha was alive (on our planet), he was having a discussion with his disciples. He asked, "Please think about it and tell me: how quickly can a person's life be taken away?" One disciple said, "People's lives can be taken away as fast as a night and a day." The Buddha shook his head and said, "Wrong!"

Another disciple said, "People's lives can be taken away as fast as the time of eating a meal!" During the time it takes to eat a meal, one's life can end. That's why Chinese people suggest: Do not invite a guest over seventy to a meal or over eighty to stay overnight. They are afraid of them choking during their meal and dying with a missed breath. So people's lives can be taken away within the time of eating one meal. But the Buddha still shook his head.

Finally, there was one disciple who said, "People's life or death are merely within a breath." The Buddha then nodded his head. One breath missed will send you to the next life!

Every one of you sitting here today are all great practitioners of the Pure Land school. The time of human life is very precious, yet very short. We should seize this fleeting time to diligently cultivate our virtue. Otherwise, with one missed breath, we will have no idea where we are heading to.

I had a classmate named Liang Donggang. He was in the same class as me during high school and college. Last year, classmates told me he had passed away from nasopharyngeal cancer. He was the same age as me. He was thirty-two years old last year. Life is so impermanent!

Twenty-Four Tests
Prove Shanti's Reincarnation True

Eventually, the case of Shanti drew hundreds of experts to investigate. They all came to the same conclusion: They admitted that this was a case of reincarnation, and that reincarnation does exist. Professor Stevenson, who we mentioned before, also personally investigated this case. His paper included this comment:

> *I also met with her father as well as related witnesses,*
> *including her former life's husband as she claimed,*
> *Kedar Nath Chaube.*
> *My investigation showed that*
> *regarding the statement of her past life,*
> *that is, the description regarding her former life,*
> *has been confirmed true at least twenty-four times.*

This means that Professor Stevenson personally conducted twenty-four tests and his investigation confirmed that her reincarnation was true.

A LIVING SOUL IN A DEAD BODY

Among the cases Professor Stevenson wrote about in the book that we mentioned before, *Twenty Cases Suggestive of Reincarnation*, there is a very special example. This case, which is also from India, is the example stated in our history as "a living soul in a dead body."

In the spring of 1954, a little boy in India named Jasbir died at the age of three. His parents were very sad as they prepared to bury him. But it was getting dark, so they thought, "Let's leave the coffin here and bury him the next morning." At midnight, the coffin began to move. This child began to wake up slowly and started to speak. His father felt very happy until he heard his three-year-old child claim that he was a twenty-two-year-old man from the village of Vehedi, a Brahmin with the surname Shankar.

Indian society is divided into many different castes. Brahmins are nobles. These noble people don't eat lower caste families' foods. Jasbir's family was a common family, so after this child woke up, he didn't want to eat his family's food. He said, "I am a Brahmin, so I cannot eat commoners' food." Fortunately, his neighbor was a Brahmin, and she cooked for him. Otherwise, he would have refused to eat and would have starved to death.

Professor Stevenson and others began to investigate the little boy. They listened to him talking about his past life. Based on his description, they found his past-life family. After verification, they confirmed that what he said was correct. This was a case of "a living soul in a dead body."

A Twenty-Two-Year-Old in a Three-Year-Old's Body

In fact, Jasbir, the three-year-old child, was dead. His soul was gone. The soul that came back to this body was actually another person. Our bodies are just like clothes. We take off one dress and put on another one. If you think the body is you and become attached to it, you will endure pointless suffering. As a matter of fact,

> *The body belongs to you and is temporarily owned by you, but it will not be in your possession permanently.*

Having such a concept, you must not become attached. Then many problems can be and will be resolved. According to the investigation, the child, after waking up, said that he was a twenty-two-year-old Brahmin youth. While he was attending a relative's wedding, another relative who owed him money had poisoned him. After he ate poisoned candy, on the way back to his house, he fell off the carriage and died. He could even remember his murderer's name! As he spoke this relative's name, he was clenching his teeth in bitter hatred.

The professors found the Brahmin's family from before his soul came to the body of this three-year-old boy. They found that there really was such a person and such an incident. That person fell from the carriage and died after attending the wedding. Many people thought that he had died from a carriage accident and didn't realize he had been murdered.

To Wish Death Upon Creditors to Escape Debt

The person who killed him in his former life had a very vicious intention—"wished death falling upon his creditor to escape debt"—it is exactly the same as stated in *Treatise on*

Response and Retribution*. He thought that he could run away and escape. Actually, he was wrong.

When one owed other people money and further took away the creditor's life, the creditor would remember and gnash his teeth every time he thought of it. We can imagine, when the enemies came face to face, their eyes would blaze with hatred. Once there was a chance, the creditor would surely retaliate. Understanding this truth, how could it be possible that one dares to do shameful things? We cannot escape from cause and effect after doing shameful things; our creditors will eventually find us.

Actually, examples of "a living soul in a dead body" are often recorded in some classical books in Chinese history, such as *A Collection of Bizarre Stories* (*Liao Zhai Zhi Yi*). Don't regard this book as merely a mythical storybook; the stories are actually true. Even *The Inner Canon of the Yellow Emperor* (*Huang Di Nei Jing*), an ancient Chinese medical text, also records the example of "a living soul in a dead body." Due to our limited time, I cannot give you a detailed report. We have to focus on Western modern scientific cases.

A THAI MONK REINCARNATED FROM HIS OWN UNCLE

Another case is also from Professor Stevenson. It is about Venerable Chao Kung, a well-respected monk in Thailand.

---

* *Treatise on Response and Retribution* is a Daoist scripture from the 12th century, very influential in China, it expounds on the relationship between cause and effect. In recent years, this Daoist scripture has been vigorously promoted by Buddhist Masters such as Master Yin Guang and Master Chin Kung.

In 1908, a relatively early time compared to now, October 12th, he was born in Surin Province, Thailand. Right after his birth, his uncle, Naileng, passed away from an illness. Please note, his uncle did not die until after he was born. Then he reincarnated as his sister's son and became Venerable Chao Kung.

His uncle in this life had been a devout Buddhist before his death. He liked to do sitting meditation every day. He was also very fond of his little sister. This little sister, named Nanleng, was now the mother of Venerable Chao Kung. When Venerable Chao Kung was very young, at the time when he began to speak, he was able to remember things from his former life. He said he knew some of his family members because he was from this family. He called his own mother "little sister" and regarded his grandmother as "mother." Obviously, this would be correct from his uncle's point of view, but from the perspective of his present life, it was wrong.

In Thailand, there is a custom that says one will encounter many misfortunes if, as a child, one remembers his/her previous life. So his family prohibited Venerable Chao Kung from talking about his past life. They forced him to forget the events of his past life.

One time, after he became a monk, a senior monk asked him, "Do you know anybody who can remember their previous lives?" Venerable Chao Kung answered, "I can remember." So he began to narrate in detail. He recalled very clearly and wrote down what he said.

Later, it was verified by Professor Stevenson. He talked about how he had been his own uncle Naileng and described in detail the process of his own death: "I (meaning Naileng), in my past life, was intermittently sick for a few months. I was lying in bed at the time when my sister was seven months pregnant. During that time, we often dreamed of each other." He stated that his sister acted very differently after becoming pregnant. She did not like to eat sour foods as in her previous pregnancies, but liked to meditate and began to have a very strong faith in Buddhism. She even became a nun during her pregnancy. In Thailand, they have short-term monastic programs.

During her ordination ceremony, Naileng, the past life of Venerable Chao Kung, said, "Although I lay in the bed, I could clearly see her ordination ceremony at the temple. I also participated!" Later, he heard his relatives talking about his little sister giving birth to a baby boy, very cute, so he decided to go and see this baby. Instead, he felt like he fell asleep. He exhaled a few heavy sighs and then closed his eyes. Actually, he had died at that moment. In other words, his last thought before death was to go take a look at the baby. After this thought, he took one last breath.

He said that he immediately recovered and felt normal again. His soul had in fact left his body at that time. To him, it seemed he had recovered his strength and was able to move around briskly. He saw that many relatives and friends had gathered around his body, crying. He told everyone, "Don't cry, you guys. I am still here, living well." But those relatives could not see nor hear him. He felt very depressed. He grabbed this person's arm, pulled that person's leg, but they all ignored him, they didn't feel anything at all. He then thought, let me go and see my little sister and her new baby.

Mortals Cannot See Spirits, but They Can See Us

You see, the soul, after leaving the body, can move about. We mortal people cannot see them, but they can see us. When we worship our ancestors, respectfully placing ancestral tablets

and chanting Amitabha, the Buddha of The Pure Land of Ultimate Bliss, they can really come and listen to our chanting.

The soul is not bound by time and space!

Two years ago, I had the honor of participating in the
opening ceremony of the All Ancestral Memorial Hall at Pure
Land Learning College in Australia. At that time, Master Chin
Kung attended the chanting in person to give this ancestral
memorial hall blessings. We were very touched when chanting
Amitabha. I remember that I was in tears while chanting Amitabha. Afterward, our mentor, Master Chin Kung told us, "You
all have really great fortune!" One of the practitioners asked,
"We are chanting Amitabha for all ancestors here. Can they
really come and listen?" Master Chin Kung nodded his head
and said, "They can really come and hear us."

It is indeed true. Now that we see these examples, we have
verified that our ancestors can really hear us and really reap the
benefits of our Amitabha recitation.

The Power of Impelling Karma

Do you recall how Naileng, the uncle of Venerable Chao
Kung, wanted to see his sister's baby? That was his last living
thought. In fact, he did go to visit the baby, who was so cute
that Naileng wanted to touch him and kiss him.

Naileng's sister saw Naileng, and she knew his body had
been cremated after death. She said to him, "Dear brother, you
have already gone to another world. Please do not appear in
front of us. Do not worry about us." She might have felt uncer-
tain when she said it, but she could really see him. At that time,
the soul of Venerable Chao Kung thought, "She is right. I must
leave. Since there are different worlds, let me go and see the
baby one more time before leaving."

When he tried to take a last glance at the baby, he felt as if he was drawn by a force. He said that some kind of spiraling force sucked him up, and soon he was unconscious. He felt like he was really dead. When he woke up later, he felt like he had become a little infant again.

> *The force that decides your destination is called*
> *"impelling karma" in Buddhism.*
> *It pulls you towards your next birth.*
> *Whatever thought that is in your mind at that moment*
> *will pull you to the place you are thinking,*
> *and then you will be reincarnated.*

Since Venerable Chao Kung was thinking of his sister's baby as he died, his soul went into the body of this little baby. For this reason, the state of mind of a dying person is extremely important.

What Appears in the World Is Only a Reflection of Our Mind

The world manifests whatever we are thinking. People who are reciting Amitabha until their death will see Amitabha in their minds. Amitabha will then lead them to be reborn into Sukhāvatī, also known as The Western Pure Land or The World of Ultimate Bliss. If you are having the thoughts of greed, resentment, or ignorance when you die, such as thinking about your house or children, then you will be reincarnated to one of the six realms: heaven, asura, human, animal, ghost, and hell. People who are reluctant to let go of their property might even become a mouse to guard their house! So we must be particularly vigilant about what we are thinking.

Venerable Chao Kung said later that he did not know how long it was until he recovered his consciousness. "But I remember that I had been Naileng not too long ago. I felt I was still this baby's uncle. I felt full of vitality." He noticed that many people talked to him and smiled at him, and he wanted to tell everybody that he was Naileng. But he could only make baby noises because he could not yet speak.

"After that, when I was preparing to wave to everyone, I was held up by my grandmother—actually my past life's mother. I wanted to call her 'Mom' because I remembered that she was my mother in my past life. But in this life, she had become my grandmother. Yet I still could not speak." After the baby could speak, there were many times that he called his own grandmother "Mom," but was corrected by the family. Because of the family's corrections, he no longer dared to mention the details of his former life.

The professors who investigated later found out that the lifestyle, expression, and attitude of Venerable Chao Kung were indeed very similar to those of his late uncle. He loved to meditate and learn about Buddhism, just like his own uncle, the man he had been in his former life. Subsequently, he became a monk in order to cultivate wisdom in this life. He was able to remember events from his former life until his old age.

This was a case of a practitioner!

Rebirth Into the Pure Land Ensures the End of Suffering

In his former life, Naileng had been a lay practitioner. In the next life, he became a monk. It is a pity that he was not seeking Pure Land rebirth due to a possibility of not encountering or not being familiar with Pure Land Buddhism, so he was again reincarnated in this world. Thanks to his good karma, he was able to clearly remember the process of his reincarnation and could even keep his human form and come back to the same family. Nonetheless, if we do not free ourselves from the cycle of birth and death—in other words, unless we are reborn into The Western Pure Land of Ultimate Bliss (Sukhāvatī)—then the suffering of reincarnation will be inevitable in the future.

Professor Stevenson, who investigated this case, acknowledged that Venerable Chao Kung had clear memories and was indeed reincarnated from Naileng. He had been his current mother's older brother and subsequently reincarnated to become his sister's son. From this case we can see that people's cultivation does not just start in this life. Venerable Chao Kung had been a practitioner in his last life who liked to meditate and learn Buddhism when he was Naileng; in this life, he became the Venerable Chao Kung, a monk in a monastery. It is actually not bad, it shows his soul was improving!

Therefore, we can deduce that so many of you here are all very devout and sincere practitioners. This did not actually begin in this life. You must have been learning Buddhism life after life!

As we have now encountered Pure Land Buddhism, we are able to seek Sukhāvatī rebirth; of course, this would not have begun in this life either. If one does not learn Pure Land Buddhism and does not vow to be reborn into The World of Ultimate Bliss (Sukhāvatī), if he practices to a certain level, he might continue learning Buddhism in his next life—but he will inevitably still suffer from the bitterness of samsara.

THE FORMER LIFE OF
CONFUCIAN MASTER WANG YANGMING

Let me share a historical story here that is similar to the studies of these Western scientists: Confucian Master Wang

Yangming was a famous scholar in the Ming Dynasty (1368–1644). You might know of him. In his time, he was well-respected by the people—and he discovered that he was reincarnated from a senior monk.

One day when he was almost fifty years old, Wang Yangming went to visit the Jinshan Temple of Zhenjiang City in Jiangsu Province. After entering the temple, he had a feeling of déjà vu. He then went walking randomly in the temple. When he approached the front door of a retreat room, he noticed that the door and windows were closed tightly, and there was even a strip of paper sealing the door. He felt that he had lived in this retreat room in the past.

He asked a monk to open the door for him, so he could enter and take a look. But the monk said, "We are really sorry, we cannot do that. You are welcome to go to any other place in the temple, but not this retreat room. Fifty years ago, the senior monk of this temple, our former abbot, went to parinirvana here. And his whole-body relic is still kept in this room. His flesh body is still sitting there and has not decayed. In order to protect this relic, we do not allow anybody to enter." But Wang Yangming was very insistent. "I implore you, I must enter and take a look." Since he was a well-known scholar and was also well-respected in the Buddhist circle, the monk finally had no choice but to let him go take a look.

Revelation at the Monastery

When the door opened, Mr. Wang stepped inside and saw an old monk sitting straight up on a meditation mat, already gone to nirvana. The true body relic was very dignified. When turning back, he saw something written on the wall. This is the poem that the abbot wrote before he went to nirvana:

> *Fifty years later Wang Yangming,*
> *the one who opens the door*
> *is the one who closed the door.*
> *The soul comes back after it had left,*
> *we then believe,*
> *the soul is really eternal*
> *like Zen Buddhism claims.*

In Buddhism, the soul refers to consciousness. People call it "soul." The abbot even gave the name of the one who would come back. From this poem, we can tell that this senior monk had genuine skills; he could predict the future and knew that he would come back fifty years later as someone named Wang Yangming! This is supernal power! But even though he possessed such an authentic skill, he still was reincarnated as Wang Yangming.

Even Great Practitioners
Can't Always Remember Previous Lives

Wang Yangming did not remember his previous life, even though he was a great practitioner and senior monk with well-respected knowledge and virtues.

Based on this story and many records throughout history, we have reason to believe that this kind of person was definitely a true practitioner in his past life. It is a pity that this senior monk did not recite Amitabha and vow to be reborn into the Pure Land. As a result, he still had to be reincarnated. With this genuine skill, if he had vowed to be reborn into the Pure Land, he would undoubtedly have ended his suffering of samsara. According to Buddhist sutras,

> *Pure Land Buddhism is a method*
> *that is extremely difficult to believe.*
> *What is the difficult part?*
> *First of all, it is very difficult to encounter.*
> *Secondly, it is also difficult to believe,*
> *even after encountering it.*

Even if someone tells you, you might still not believe in it and not be willing to recite Amitabha at the moment of death. As such, suffering from reincarnation is inevitable. And it will cause confusion between the two lives. Even returning bodhisattvas* would possibly forget the experiences of their past lives, just like this senior monk. It really is a pity because those skills he had cultivated were all interrupted.

In this life, we have encountered our teacher, Master Chin Kung, who introduced Pure Land Buddhism so clearly to us; this is truly hard to encounter, even in thousands of billions of kalpas*. We should seize this opportunity and achieve the monumental task of liberating ourselves from the cycle of birth and death in this life.

---

*Generally speaking, a bodhisattva is a Buddhist practitioner intent on the attainment of enlightenment based on profoundly altruistic motivations. "Bodhi" means "enlightenment," and "sattva" means "living being." Thus, a being who has been awakened and seeks enlightenment, or an enlightened being is called a bodhisattva. A bodhisattva who dedicates his or her efforts to the salvation of other beings is the model practitioner in the Mahāyāna tradition.

*Kalpa: a Sanskrit word for the longest period of time in the Indian cosmology—the period of time between the creation and re-creation of a world or universe. It is an unimaginably long unit of time.

WHERE REINCARNATION AND
BIOLOGY INTERSECT

Let's return to our subject and continue to explore the proofs of Western science. Professor Stevenson's scientific proofs of these cases of reincarnation have been appreciated by the American and Western medical community, so we will look at more of his cases. He not only reported many cases of reincarnation but also concluded some theories from these cases. Let's explore those theories, which are published in his book *Where Reincarnation and Biology Intersect.* In this book, Professor Stevenson integrated biology and reincarnation, using them to explain each other.

Story One:
Reincarnation of the Pollock Twins

The Pollock twins were born in October 1958 in England. Between the time when they were two and four years old, they were able to remember their past lives as their two deceased sisters, Joanna and Jacqueline.

Joanna and Jacqueline Pollock had been eleven and six years old when they died in a tragic car accident on May 5, 1957. A car drove onto the sidewalk and killed these two girls. At the beginning of the second year after their death, 1958, their mother was pregnant again. Their father had a strange thought: without rhyme nor reason, he said that she would deliver twins this time. The doctor denied that Mrs. Pollock was pregnant with twins, but the father insisted otherwise. He was correct. Mrs. Pollock gave birth to twins and named them Gillian and Jennifer.

Proof of the Reincarnation
as Their Own Younger Sisters

When these twins were two or three years old, they claimed that they were the two sisters who had died in this family. Investigators tested them; for example, when the twins were given the toys of their deceased sisters, they would retrieve their own favorite toys of their previous life. The older one would retrieve the older sister's toys, and the younger twin would retrieve the younger sister's toys. They would identify their toys by the made-up names the two deceased sisters had given them.

Once, while the family was driving through an area where the little girls had never been in this life, they suddenly pointed to a building and shouted out: "Hey, that is the school we studied at before!" They both seemed to recognize it, even though they were still too young to go to school. Both claimed they had studied in this school before, and they even described some swings in the back of the school where they often played. Everything they said matched details from the lives of their deceased sisters.

Learning Capabilities
Are Retained Between Lives

Joanna, the older sister of the deceased sisters, had loved to teach her younger sister to write. In this life, Gillian, the older twin, learned very quickly to hold a pen and to write, while the younger twin struggled to hold a pen correctly. She clasped the pen in her fist, as the younger deceased sister had.

In this life, the older twin was a fast learner and the younger twin learned more slowly. This also was related to their past lives. The learning capabilities of people vary. Some people seem to be especially smart, learning things quickly, while others struggle to learn. That is related to their past lives.

When one seems to learn something particularly fast, he might be remembering some of the training from a past life. Otherwise, how can you explain someone like Mozart, a musical genius who began composing large, complex symphonies before he turned six years old? The explanation is that learning acquired in past lives sometimes carries over. This kind of person was probably a musician in their past life already, and his genius had been retained. Beethoven was the same way. Both musicians died early, but their musical talent was evident during childhood.

Birthmarks Can Be Passed on Life After Life

These twins were both born with birthmarks in the same locations as their deceased sisters. A birthmark might stay with a person for several lives, and other physical characteristics such as appearance might also be the same over several lifetimes. Some people were born good-looking, probably because they have done good deeds in their past life. A good heart brings a better-looking appearance. On the contrary, if the heart is evil, this evil heart can create an ugly appearance that lasts for lifetimes.

Story Two: Lulao's Prophecy and Proof

Let me tell you another story that is recorded in official Chinese history. In the Tang Dynasty, there was a person named

Cui Xian from Shandong Province. He grew up with noble aspirations and was highly educated. In the first year of the Yuanhe era of Emperor Xianzong, this young man passed the two highest levels of imperial exams, Juren and Jinshi, in the same year. His official career reached the high-ranking position of "Shiyushi," similar to today's position of a general prosecutor. He was specifically in charge of prosecuting criminal cases. With a charismatic personality, Cui Xian was a righteous person and was very smart at making decisions with criminal cases, he earned the reputation of being guarded by deities because he dealt with those cases like a god and was very accurate.

Cui Xian's father was Cui Rui, also an imperial officer. During his official career, of course, he was a very kind person who greatly respected the saints and sages. One day, a practitioner came to his house. This practitioner called himself "Lulao" (Mandarin pronunciation, meaning Senior Lu). This Lulao had reached a very high level in his practice—he could predict the future and know the past. Cui Rui respected Lulao and invited him to stay at his home. After a period of time, Lulao told Cui Rui it was time for him to leave. He said, "I am leaving, but we have a very deep affinity in the future. After I finish this life, I will reincarnate into your family and become your son. There will be proof!" "What will that be?" Cui Rui asked. Lulao pointed to a mole beneath his mouth and said, "This will be our proof." He left after giving his word.

Later, Cui Rui had a son, Cui Xian. Sure enough, he had a birthmark: a mole beneath his mouth. His son also grew up to look and act like Lulao. So his father nicknamed him "Lulao," to commemorate this practitioner.

Suffering in the Womb Causes Us to Forget Our Previous Life

We can see from this case, if we don't cultivate and vow to be reborn into the Pure Land—even if we are so advanced that we have a genuine skill of predicting the future and knowing the past, just like Lulao—we will still be reincarnated within the six realms. Only by cultivating The Pure Land Method and seeking rebirth to The World of Ultimate Bliss (Sukhāvatī) can we escape the cycle of birth and death.

After reincarnation, most people forget their past life—unless they are like Venerable Chao Kung, the Thai example we mentioned earlier.

The reason he remembered his prior life is because he did not go through the suffering of the prison-like pain of being carried in a womb as the Buddha Dharma states. He did not suffer the months of pain because he did not actually enter his mother's womb. Instead, he entered the baby's body after the child was born. At the moment of his death he was thinking of the baby, so his consciousness went to the baby at the moment of his death. From this case we can easily comprehend that the power of the mind is inconceivable. It can create our world! Buddha Dharma states,

> *Our world is "manifested by the heart*
> *and altered by consciousness."*
> *This is especially true at the moment of our death.*
> *The moment of death is the time of altering our realm,*
> *entering a different world.*

That interval of time when we are near death is particularly critical. Whatever you are thinking of will appear in front of you. Venerable Chao Kung was thinking of his sister's baby, and subsequently went to the baby's body and became her son. He retained all his memories because he did not endure the extreme suffering of hanging upside-down in a mother's womb.

I saw a documentary film produced by the American Discovery channel in Hong Kong when I was on the way here. Thanks to the advanced technology nowadays, film producers used a three-dimensional ray to film the complete activities of a baby inside a mother's womb, so we were able to see the baby's suffering. Being soaked in the amniotic fluid in the mother's womb and hung upside down for ten months must be a distressing torment. During this suffering, a baby will forget the events of his previous life. The pain drives out his memories. Consequently, few people can remember their past lives. Only those who did not experience this suffering might remember.

Stories Three and Four:
Professor Stevenson's Birthmark Theory

Professor Stevenson proposed a theory that birthmarks are related to one's former life. He used a biological perspective to talk about this issue. Another more recent case of his from the United States is even more convincing:

A Birthmark
Caused by Last Life's Car Crash

Winnie, a very cute four-year-old girl, died in a car accident in 1961. Of course, her family was very sad. The husband

and wife, and their other daughter, the older sister of this deceased girl, were all immersed in grief.

About six months after Winnie's death, Winnie's older sister, also a little girl, suddenly dreamed that Winnie would be coming back home. Her mother became pregnant after this incident! During the pregnancy, her mother also dreamed that Winnie said she would be coming back to reunite with the family. Her mother gave birth in 1964. In front of the delivery room, her father heard Winnie's voice. He reported it was a very clear voice, not dreamlike. He clearly heard Winnie say, "Dad, I am coming back." Then the baby was born. This baby was also a girl and was given the name Susan.

When Susan was two years old, she began to talk about having been a girl named Winnie. She liked two pictures of Winnie. She pointed to one and said, "This person is me." She put one picture on the headboard of her bed and carried the other with her and cherished it. Susan often repeated sentences beginning with "when I was in school…," and then started to chat with her parents about her past. Professor Stevenson later confirmed the truth of the events that Susan mentioned.

Interestingly, there was a large birthmark on the left side of Susan's hip. This birthmark corresponded exactly to the wound left by her deceased sister's car accident. Professor Stevenson went to the hospital where Winnie died after the car accident and examined the autopsy chart to verify that the injured part of Winnie's body was consistent with the birthmark Susan had in this life.

Based on cases like this, Professor Stevenson believes that if a person died from certain kinds of trauma—a sharp blade, a puncture wound, or impact—the injured area would leave a birthmark on later reincarnations. He used more than 200 cases that he investigated to confirm his theory.

Birthmark of a Bullet Wound
and the Memory of Past Life Death

Professor Stevenson introduced the case of an Indian boy who remembered his own previous life in a village in India. In this past life, his name had been Maha. He was murdered when someone shot a bullet that passed through his chest. The position of the bullet passing through is shown in the autopsy report (diagram on the left) that Professor Stevenson found in the hospital.

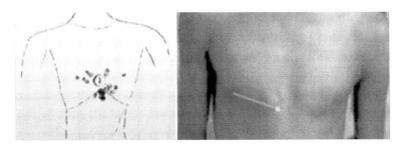

The right side picture is this Indian boy who claimed that he could remember his previous life, including the way he died. He was born with a birthmark which was indeed like a bullet wound.

Physical and Mental Trauma
Can Be Passed on to the Next Life

From studying more than 200 similar cases, Professor Stevenson developed two theories, which he described to me. It was the time after I finished my studies in the United States, I contacted him while I was teaching at the University of Texas. The professor told me about his birthmark theory—birthmarks in this lifetime can show the position of mortal wounds from a previous lifetime—he also believes that our talents carry over into future lives.

by coincidence: the professor ordered a parrot she had never seen to be delivered through the postal service. However,

> *The causal conditions between sentient beings,*
> *in reality, are not accidental.*

It was not just by chance that she would bring the parrot home by ordering it casually through the mail,

> *It was actually "an inevitable karmic attraction."*

The karmic relationships between us and sentient beings around us are determined by past lives. The Buddha taught us that there are only four relationships among people:

> *Collecting debt, repaying debt,*
> *returning debt of gratitude, and seeking revenge.*

AREA THREE:
REINCARNATION STUDIES
USING HYPNOSIS

We have looked at research attempting to prove the existence of the soul, and studies of people who spontaneously remember details of their past lives. Some Western doctors and psychological experts use hypnotic methods to help their patients remember their past lives.

Hypnosis is translated into Chinese as "expediting sleep," which I think is not very accurate—because hypnosis actually is not a sleeping state. The brain waves of sleep and hypnosis are completely different. What state of mind is hypnosis, really? During hypnosis, a doctor or psychiatrist helps the patient relax to enter a relatively deep and stable mental state. So, being under hypnosis is quite a bit like the meditation state. In this highly concentrated state of spirit, the hypnotized person feels peaceful. Sometimes, a hypnotized person can recall incidents from far in their past.

This hypnotic method was invented by doctors of psychology who used it to help patients find the root cause of their symptoms. The doctors assumed that the root cause was from experiences in the patient's childhood, a sequela from a mental trauma that left psychological barriers. Their theory is that recalling the traumatic incidents can help the patient settle their mind and recover to normal.

Some doctors who use hypnosis found that, unexpectedly, their patients would remember details of their former lives. This ignited reincarnation research through the method of hypnosis. The number of people who engage in such research is considerable, it includes experts, professors, and outpatient doctors in the psychiatry and psychology fields. Some of the more influential people using hypnosis to study reincarnation include a vice-president of The American Society for Psychical Research—Dr. C.J. Ducasse, a well-known professor at Brown University—as well as Dr. Helen Wambach, Dr. Edith Fiore, Dr. R. Woolger, Dr. Rick Brown, and Dr. Brian Weiss. These people have become famous because of the results of their work.

HYDROPHOBIA DUE TO
DROWNING IN A PREVIOUS LIFE

Dr. Rick Brown reported on an American salesman who had a psychological illness. Dr. Brown was the vice president of The International Association for Regression Research & Therapies and a famous psychiatrist who used hypnosis to help patients recover.

The hypnotic method can be effective in helping patients recognize the cause of their mental illness, which might help them release their traumas. Hypnosis sometimes has an almost magical effect on the treatment of these mental illnesses, and even on physical illnesses. A type of hypnosis called "regression therapy" helps patients recall their past by gradually directing the patient's attention backwards in time.

The case of the salesman was published in *The International Journal of Regression Therapy* (Issue 5, 1991, p. 62—71). This salesman developed hydrophobia when he was thirty-four years old. Patients with hydrophobia are afraid of water. In extreme cases, hydrophobics are too afraid to swim, step onto a boat, or even go into a bathtub. This patient's fear of water was so serious that it interfered with his job; he found himself unable to travel because of this mental illness. He turned to Dr. Brown for hypnosis to help him determine the cause of this fear.

I have used a CD to perform self-hypnosis, and it seems to work pretty well. But hypnotic therapists are specifically trained so they can help to guide patients to a focused yet very tranquil state of mind. In some cases, this state enables them to remember a former life.

Dying on a Submarine Called "Shark" During World War II

Under Dr. Brown's guidance, this patient recalled his past life as an American sailor on a submarine called "Shark" during World War II. His name then had been Jim. Research later confirmed that this submarine did exist. On February 11,

1942, while at war with Japan in the ocean off Manila, Philippines, the submarine was hit and sunk by a Japanese destroyer. The attack killed all of the American sailors, including Jim.

Dr. Brown recorded an audio tape of the patient as he began to recall his past life as Jim. He said that morning, on the day of the disaster, the waters near Manila were tranquil. Their submarine was completing assignments under the sea when suddenly, an alarm went off. Jim heard a siren loudly blaring in the cabin. The crew had spotted a Japanese destroyer fleet ahead.

The U.S. Military and Japanese Army were enemies at that time, so the submarine's crew prepared to fight. In the meantime, the Japanese fleet also spotted the U.S. submarine, and they attacked first by shooting torpedoes at the U.S. submarine. The first torpedo struck the submarine's tail, and the vessel started to shake violently. The patient under hypnosis saw the whole scene. He said that he felt the entire submarine shaking. The lights in the submarine went off and then slowly lit up again. The submarine was a total mess. Sailors were rushing to grab their life jackets and some were preparing to return fire. The sound of the alarm and the screaming plunged the cabin into chaos.

Very quickly, a second torpedo hit the submarine. This time, it struck right on target, tearing a gaping hole through the vessel's hull. Because the submarine was submerged at the time, seawater poured into the cabin. Jim said he could feel the freezing seawater rapidly rising in the cabin. Before he could grab a life jacket, the submarine was engulfed by the icy sea. The whole crew of U.S. military officers and sailors drowned before the submarine sank to the bottom of the sea.

After finishing this hypnosis treatment, Dr. Brown, based on the records from the recording, went to the U.S. Military Archives to verify this incident. Was there really such an incident? Yes, his visit had helped him to ascertain that there was indeed a U.S. submarine called "Shark." In 1942, it was hit by a Japanese destroyer and sank to the ocean floor. His researchers also found a sailor named Jim on the list of casualties. It was verified! This patient was not talking nonsense; he was remembering a past life.

This case tells us that our souls are indeed reincarnated, and even after the memories of reincarnation fade, under certain conditions, we can recall details of our past lives—through hypnosis! Many Americans and Westerners like to experience hypnosis. Some of them are curious, and some want to know what was going on in their past lives. In Buddhism, people who practice meditation can also see their own past lives. These can all serve as proof of reincarnation.

**Regression Therapy
Cures Mental Illnesses**

After his regression therapy, the salesman found that his fear of water slowly subsided. Hypnosis has often been successful in helping patients overcome such psychological barriers.

Buddhism can help us understand why this method is effective: The incidents of our past are as illusionary as a dream or a bubble—yet deep down in our souls, we still cling to the emotions of the incident. We sometimes allow things that caused us pain in the past to torment our present spirits or even our physical bodies. This can be the basis of mental disorder. When we relax and let go of the attachment, our mental illness will slowly get better. The most critical step is to *awaken.*

All Things Are as Illusory
as a Dream, Bubble, or Shadow

We must realize that the past is just a dream or a bubble. As a matter of fact, everything in our present time is *also* illusory, like a dream or a bubble. Don't think that only the things in our past have passed. In fact, we are constantly changing in every moment of the present; the you of this hour and the next hour are different; even the you of this second and the next are different. In other words, the whole universe of this second and the next are different—because the universe is the manifestation of our mind. Since thoughts continuously come in and out of our minds, every second is different. On this account, the universe manifested by our mind is different every second. In the *Diamond Sutra,* there is a very famous teaching:

> *All conditioned phenomena*
> *are just as illusory as a dream, bubble, or shadow,*
> *and as momentary as morning dew or lightning,*
> *they should be regarded as such.*

The Buddha taught us to observe all phenomena of the universe like this. Every thought is different. The dharma-realm manifested by one thought is one universe, and the universe of this thought is different from the universe contrived by the next thought. Therefore, each dharma-realm is different.

So where is anything real?

All objects in the universe are manifested by thoughts. Since they are manifested, they are not real. They cannot exist eternally. The time of their existence is only within one thought. That's why it is said, "As illusory as a dream, bubble, or shadow, and as momentary as morning dew or lightning."

But why do we seem to see the existence now?

What we are seeing is all causes and conditions coming together.

Yet, the causes and conditions do not *really* come together. They are not truly together because they are constantly changing—as illusory as a dream, a bubble, or a shadow. If we can truly comprehend this, all of our psychological disorders will be resolved. We think some patients have intense psychological disorders, but actually we all have psychological delusions—because we have not understood the *truth* of reality yet. As long as we still have attachment, we will have suffering, we are not normal.

Only if we let go of attachment, can we then let go of suffering. The more attachment we release, the less suffering we will feel.

Only Buddhas are completely free from psychological delusions, so they are completely normal. Before we become a Buddha, we are all abnormal to some extent; worse than those better ones, yet better than those worse ones.

THE PROTAGONIST OF
MANY LIVES, MANY MASTERS

Dr. Brian Weiss, a famous psychiatrist, is the president of the Miami Mt. Sinai Medical Center. He graduated from the prestigious Yale Medical School in the United States in 1970 and received a medical doctorate degree. He taught at the University of Pittsburgh and Miami University, and he has accumulated more than thirty years of experience in psychological clinical care.

Dr. Weiss has published a large number of papers and works regarding his experiences in the modern psychological and spiritual field, particularly in the field of the study of reincarnation. His masterpiece is *Many Lives, Many Masters.* This book has been translated into many languages, including Chinese. Dr. Weiss also wrote *Through Time Into Healing,* and *Mirrors of Time.* He developed hypnotic methods to help his patients recall their past lives in order to treat their psychological disorders. Now he is considered the most famous and authoritative expert on the use of hypnosis to help people recall their past lives and resolve any psychological disorders that have arisen from those experiences. He has collected many cases.

When I was in the United States, I once contacted Dr. Weiss by phone. At that time, our mentor, Master Chin Kung, hoped to spread Western science to prove the existence of reincarnation. So he asked me to contact Dr. Weiss, hoping to invite him to our Hong Kong studio to record a speech in English on VCD, specifically for Westerners. Dr. Weiss told me that he had treated more than 20,000 cases in a few decades, and these patients could all remember their past lives. Unfortunately, he said, he was now too busy, because people all around the world had invited him to give speeches on reincarnation. His schedule had been booked for two years, and there was no way that he could fit the time in. We had no choice but to give up on our recording project.

Dr. Weiss is a very nice, loving person. He hopes to spread the truth that has been confirmed by science to the people of the world. I am going to introduce to you his most famous case and his first book, *Many Lives, Many Masters*, which some of you have already read.

Mental Depression
Cured by Regression Therapy

Many Lives, Many Masters is a book written by Dr. Weiss about one of his cases. In 1980, a female laboratory technician at the Miami Medical Center, where Dr. Weiss worked, asked him for help. He called her "Catherine."

Catherine did not have much education and was a simple and honest person. She grew up in a Catholic family where there was never any talk about reincarnation. When she was twenty-seven, she had a boyfriend named Stuart. Whenever she was with him, she always had a strange feeling, like something wasn't right. As they spent more time together, this feeling became troublesome.

Catherine was suffering from mental depression, a condition that is common today. She felt nervous and anxious, she had frequent nightmares, and she even began sleepwalking. Her condition was quite serious. She developed fear of the dark and fear of being in a confined space. She had severe claustrophobia and felt too uncomfortable to fly in an airplane. She was also terrified of water, often fearing she would choke even when she took medicine with water. All day she was worried that she was going to die. These were her mental conditions at the time.

Dr. Weiss used a number of traditional methods to treat her, yet they had no effect. Finally, he used hypnosis to help her to recall her past, in the hope of finding the cause of her psychological barriers.

Recalling More Than Ten Past Lives While Under Hypnosis

Unexpectedly, Catherine recalled more than ten past reincarnations during those hypnotic processes. She was able to describe many events of those lives in detail, including the times and places she lived and the names of the people she knew. Dr. Weiss was convinced these were not delusions or fiction she made up. He organized the tape recordings of her hypnosis and later published them.

During the hypnosis treatment, Catherine said she had reincarnated on this Earth eighty-six times over about 4,000 to 5,000 years.

What lives had she lived? Some had been tragic; she was a female slave in ancient Egypt, a prostitute under the kingdom of a Spanish colony in the 18th century, and a woman living in a cave in the ancient Stone Age. She also remembered being a slave in Virginia of the United States in the 19th century. She struggled with many difficulties in these lives. In her latest life, she was a male German pilot who was killed in France during World War II.

Dr. Weiss hypnotized her more than ten times, and each time, she described each of her major reincarnations in much more detail than I am supplying here.

The True Nature of One's Hidden Self

During one of her hypnosis treatments, Catherine described seeing a big, white building with steps but no doors. She had regressed to the Egyptian era. She said she was a slave helping to build an Egyptian pyramid by hauling sand. She said, "My name is Aronda. I'm twenty-five years old now." She said that the year was 1862 BC. That was a long time ago, in an era earlier than the lives of Shakyamuni Buddha and Confucius!

"I have a little daughter named Kleyastra," she said. "She is my niece now."

She was able to observe how her relationship with this girl had spanned two incarnations, being her daughter of her past life and her niece in this life. She and her niece had a very good relationship, like mother and daughter—because they had been mother and daughter in a past life!

This patient said, "We lived in a village, inside a very dry valley where it was very hot. Suddenly one day, from the mountain, water rushed down and flooded the valley abruptly, like a tsunami. The flood submerged our village. Many trees were overturned. Everyone was fleeing." She remembered holding her daughter Kleyastra tightly and wanting to escape. But a big wave rushed in and submerged them both. Her daughter was torn out of her arms. She felt she was choking, uncomfortable, and unable to breathe.

Manifested by the Heart and Altered by Consciousness

As she described the situation, Catherine's hands clutched the air, as if she was really submerged in water. You see, when this patient entered the hypnotic state, she was completely in that realm. The doctor saw the situation and was afraid she might really choke, so he quickly gave her instructions, "You are now relaxed. You are safe now, and this incident has all passed. You can relax and rest." The patient slowly calmed down and her breathing eased.

This can actually give us a lot of inspiration! The scene that the patient saw during hypnosis was not seen by the doctor—yet she became immersed in it. Her whole body and spirit went into that environment, as if she felt the flood submerging her and her daughter being torn away. She was very sad.

When she was in that realm, what created her realm? It was created by her thoughts. Accordingly, we should be able to comprehend the revelation from the Dharma:

> *The world is manifested by the heart*
> *and altered by consciousness.*

Whatever thoughts we have, a corresponding realm will be shown to us. It is truly like this! So, if we think of Amitabha, The Pure Land of Ultimate Bliss (Sukhāvatī) will be manifested, without a doubt at all.

Our Root-Nature Can See Past Lives

Thus we said, the six roots of all beings—eye, ear, nose, tongue, body, and consciousness—have their root-nature. This story can help us comprehend it. Picture this patient describing the flood, yet the doctor did not see the flood. She lay on the bed with her eyes closed—so what did she use to see the flood? Think about it, everyone:

Did she use her eyes to see? Her eyes were closed!

Buddha Dharma states that each of our six roots all has its own root-nature, and we can use our root-nature to see. The patient can see the past and the present time under hypnosis because the hypnotic, tranquil state is similar to dhyana—a sanskrit word which refers to a deep meditation—allowing her vision-nature to function. Since the vision-nature does not differentiate between past or future times, she could see the past under hypnosis. However, when one is deluded, giving rise to many wandering thoughts, his vision-nature will become eye-consciousness—and that will become an obstacle for one to see the past or future.

One's True-Nature Is
Beyond Life and Death

Can people really neither be born nor die?

Can we really escape from the sufferings of samsara?

We must understand that people truly have something that is neither birth nor death, so of course they can neither be born nor die. If we want to end our reincarnation, we only need to find the things that have no reincarnation. Then we will be free from samsara. What things have no reincarnation? Among our six roots (eye, ear, nose, tongue, body, and consciousness), the things with no reincarnation are hidden—that is the nature of these roots.

The root-nature has no reincarnation, and it neither arises nor ceases.

Dr. Weiss' patient Catherine saw the situation of her past, which proves that our vision-nature does not distinguish between past or future. It can see the past, it can see the present, and it can see the future as well. It can see this place, it can also see other places. The universe is vast, yet our vision-nature can see everywhere in the void of all dharma-realms; this is its function. All things in the entire universe have this vision-nature. So, from the perspective of vision-nature, the universe is truly one entity. This nature has no reincarnation; in Buddhism, it is called the true-body, true-me, or self-nature. Actually it means "the truth," which we will explore later.

The Heart
Is the Master of All Things

When the hypnotized patient Catherine saw the water flooding her village, she died—she died in that life. She slowly returned to normal under the doctor's guidance. After this treatment, her hydrophobia disappeared. She recovered, because she now understood that cause. She became normal!

The mind is the master of our bodies and spirit. However, our mind is dominated by delusions, so our spirit and thinking are still not the *noumenon*—something that exists independent from our perception. Once we really understand this, we are awakened! Once awakened, we will then truly let go of our attachments and delusional thoughts.

In other words, we will recover to "normal"! For instance, the patient's fear of water was a delusional thought; she became normal once she let go of it.

The Hidden Messages in Water

Japanese scientist Dr. Masaru Emoto proved through his water experiments that the heart is the master of all things. This is one of Dr. Masaru Emoto's research results:

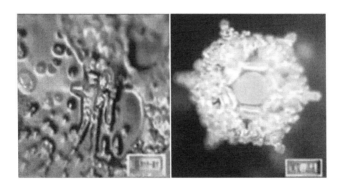

He took two glasses of water, and on one glass he taped a paper with the writing of "disgusting, really annoying, I want to kill you"—various vicious words. He labeled the other glass of water with wonderful words such as "love" or "thankful." After a period of time, he used a high-power microscope to observe how the water would crystallize in cold temperatures. As a result, the water crystals were different. The water crystals from the glass with the vicious language were like the left picture above, very ugly. The water glass with the words of "love" and "gratitude" produced crystals like the right side picture above, symmetric and beautiful.

Dr. Masaru Emoto's scientific experiment proves that the heart is able to affect the material structure of an object.

Our Heart Can Protect the Environment

But how can this work?

Vicious words are generated from an unwholesome heart, yet love and gratitude come from a kind heart. The thoughts from a kind heart can turn the water into a beautiful crystal. In other words,

Our heart/mind can change the structure of substances.

We know that 70 percent of our bodies are water and 70 percent of our Earth is also covered by the water of the ocean, rivers, and so on. If everyone had a good heart, we could heal our bodies and also protect our environment!

It is wonderful that there are so many Pure Land Societies in Taiwan. We are here in Liuhe Pure Land Society today, where so many good practitioners chant Amitabha together; this Buddha name of Amitabha that we recite must have created very beautiful crystals in the water of our body, our environment, as well as our Earth.

Our words, prompted by love,
can truly eliminate and free us from disasters!

Buried Alive

In another course of treatment, Dr. Weiss' patient Catherine cured another psychological symptom. She was afraid of darkness, afraid of the feeling of being closed in a confined space. Under hypnosis, she recalled an incarnation a long, long time ago as a person who lived in an ancient tribe. The tribe was overrun by plague. Once a person was infected, death was unavoidable—it was similar to the bird flu we have now.

People in the tribe at that time thought the plague was a punishment from God. Instead of receiving care, victims were immediately brought to a cave in the mountains, which was then sealed with soil. They were buried alive and died inside. Catherine became infected with this plague. She was carried to the cave and buried in dirt.

She recalled feeling hopeless. In the dark cave, she was very scared, very desperate. She finally died in a state of despair and fear. This manifested as a trauma in her present life, deep in her heart; that's why she was scared of being enclosed in a dark space and was afraid of dark rooms. Under the doctor's guidance, once she understood the root cause, she slowly recovered to normal.

From a Murderer to a Boyfriend

In one of Catherine's hypnosis sessions, she recalled the situation of another life when she became a boy! In the hypnotic state, she said, "I have blond hair. We are having a battle on the water. I see many white warships and many of our people are holding long spears, bows and arrows, as well as shields. We are fighting against the enemy." At that time, this boy was scared. He held a knife in his hand, but he did not go up to fight with the enemy because he did not want to kill people.

Right after she described the situation, Catherine, who was lying on a bed in the hypnotic state, suddenly seemed to have difficulty breathing. After a while, she slowly told the situation. She said that an enemy rushed to him from behind, strangled his neck with his hand, and then used a knife to slit his throat.

When he was dying, the boy turned around and saw the enemy. She said she recognized him: he was her boyfriend in this life. She said that his appearance was completely different, yet she knew that it was him.

Destiny Makes Enemies Meet

This life of Catherine reminds us of the proverb, "Destiny makes enemies meet." Mutual injuries are avenged on each other, life after life. An invisible force of karma entwines two people together. So the relationships among people are none other than

> *paying a debt of gratitude, seeking revenge,*
> *collecting debt, and repaying debt.*

If you took someone's life in a past incarnation, then the two of you will become entangled together to return the debt. We see so many problems in society such as husband and wife not getting along and disharmony among family members, resulting in a high divorce rate and an unstable society. Most of these problems have causes from their past lives.

Let me show you a few figures: In 2002, the number of divorces in the U.S. was 800,000. This is an alarmingly high number! In China, the statistics in 2003 showed there were

1.33 million couples divorced. These numbers are astonishing, and in most countries, the rate is increasing!

Why do couples not get along? This can be attributed to the cause and effect of their past lives. To turn enemies into family members requires some great lessons! Just understanding that the divorce of a husband and wife may be attributed to the cause and effect of their past lives will still not mend the problem.

Sage Education Can
Turn Past Enemies Into Family

If understanding the cause isn't enough, how can we resolve these problems? Honestly, we can only rely on sage education, as our master advocates. Sage education focuses on the moral teachings of traditional Chinese culture. It strongly emphasizes being filial to parents and being fraternal to siblings, then further extending this love and respect to all elders as well as others' parents and siblings.

The sage education can turn past enemies into families.

Sages transform relationships through sincere love. Only sincere love can transform people. Yet where does the sincere love come from? Our mentor, Master Chin Kung said, "It has to rely on *education*." People have an inherently good nature. However, our society contains so much pollution that one's little goodness will quickly wear off. Therefore, when we forsake sage education, society will remain in turmoil—the high divorce rate is a sign of social unrest, a harbinger of disasters, so we must be vigilant.

Lately, Master Chin Kung has been preparing to go to Indonesia to participate in an international religious conference. He was invited to give a keynote speech on the topic "Compassion, Fraternity, Sincerity, Respect, Humility, and Harmony." This subject summarizes the sage teachings. If we really encounter our past lives' enemies, we should use these six qualities. We should endure, show generosity, and even sacrifice and dedicate ourselves to resolve their resentment toward us. Only by using this method can we transform the relationships with them.

We Must First Resolve the Grievance in Our Own Heart

With so much resentment and disaster in the world, where do we start to resolve it? Our Master said, "To resolve resentments, we must resolve our own heart first." We must resolve our inner grievances, conflicts, and resentments. We must let go of all these bad thoughts and remove them from our heart. Then we can begin to resolve other people's resentments. We do not know what kind of relationship we had with the people around us in past lives, but it can all be resolved, no matter what it was.

Look at Emperor Shun*, who was known for using his great filial piety to resolve the resentment his stepmother had for him. We know Shun's stepmother kept trying to kill him; this must have had a past life's causality, or else why would she always try to murder her own stepson for no reason? Although he wasn't her biological son, she had no reason to kill him.

---

*Shun was a legendary leader of ancient China, best known for his filial piety toward his stepmother and sincere fraternity toward his stepbrothers. He not only transformed his entire family but touched the Emperor of that time, Yao, to pass down the throne to him.

But Emperor Shun used these virtues—Compassion, Fraternity, Sincerity, Respect, Humility, and Harmony—along with his persistent forbearance to finally influence and reform his parents. He became the number one example of "The 24 Filial Piety Stories" in Chinese history. Confucius praised filial piety most highly. Mencius also said, "The Dao (Way) of Emperor Yao* and Shun is simply filial piety and fraternity." Therefore,

Only sage education can help us to resolve problems.

Cause and effect help us to recognize the problem, we talk about causal reincarnation today to help us recognize the problem. But to solve the problem, we must rely on sage education.

The Fetus Is Indeed a Life

After this patient, Catherine, was killed in that life—killed by her present life's boyfriend—she described that her soul floated away from her body and drifted into the air. And then she was drawn by an invisible force, drawn into a very narrow but warm space; she had entered her mother's womb. Soon, she would be reborn to her next life.

From her description, we can see that, at the moment of entering the womb during the process of transmigration, the

---

*Emperor Yao was one of the Five Legendary Emperors in ancient Chinese history. He lived around 2200 BC. Being moved by Shun's filial piety and compassion, Emperor Yao passed down his throne to Shun, which was honored as "A Politics of Conceding the Throne" and was admired by Chinese people from generation to generation.

soul is obviously aware. After entering the womb, due to the suffering, one then forgets his past life. Thus we say, "The fetus itself is indeed a life."

Many people nowadays have the medical misconception that the fetus is still not life and can be called life only after giving birth. This is a fallacy from the point of view of reincarnation. A fetus itself already has all of the features of a person. If you observe the photos of a fetus, the five sensory organs are complete. Eyes, ears, nose, tongue, body, and consciousness are all there. Even the soul is there. It is a complete life. Hence, abortion is exactly the same as murdering a person, and

> *It is not only killing an ordinary person*
> *but killing your own child.*
> *For this reason,*
> *the sin of abortion is especially serious.*

The Number of Abortions Worldwide Is Skyrocketing

Abortion is a very critical social problem nowadays. I want to emphasize this issue more. Let me show you some staggering figures. According to the message from "Population Network," there are one billion youth in the world between the ages of fifteen to twenty-four, of whom about *five million* have had abortions.

What is the concept of this number? We know that the populations of Taipei and Kaohsiung (the two largest cities in Taiwan) combined are less than five million—yet there have been five million abortions. Some reports speculate that, on average, there are ten young girls getting an abortion every minute—that is about one abortion every six seconds. Before I finish the sentence I am speaking, another life will have been brutally taken away.

In the United States, doctors perform 1.5 million surgical abortions per year. In Taiwan, there are half a million abortions every year. These figures are really disturbing and hard to believe. After ten years, the entire population of Taipei and Kaohsiung would have been wiped out. It is horrendous!

These lives have souls!

Since we know that they have souls, how heavy would their resentment be after they are killed? So it is inevitable that our planet would have these big disasters. That is, the grievances of these aborted baby spirits indeed will bring our world immeasurable disasters.

Every day, when we are reciting Amitabha, we should transfer the merits to these innocent victims, these hundreds of millions of infant spirits. If they do not get salvation, their grievances will not let those of us who are still alive be free from disasters. You all have great merit by reciting Amitabha. It can really help to eliminate disasters.

The Horrors of Abortion

Abortion can really cause serious harm to a person. One American woman said that when she finished the abortion, the doctor showed her the results of his successful procedures: a keg loaded with the infant's broken body parts including a head, hands, even fingers. She saw them all clearly, all smashed into debris. This mother said her heart began trembling as she realized that she had killed her own child.

She became mentally ill after the abortion, often trying to end her own life.

A male doctor at a private clinic in the United States said he performed fifty to sixty abortion procedures each day, on average. One day, he said, he entered his office and saw a long line of young women waiting for abortions and thought, "I received a doctorate degree in medicine because I wanted to serve female patients. I would never have expected that I would have to take so many lives." His conscience suddenly caught up with him. He said that he would never dare to perform an abortion again.

The World That Accumulates Evil Will Have Many Disasters

> *The family that accumulates goodness*
> *is sure to have abundant blessings.*
> *And the family that accumulates evil*
> *is sure to have abundant misery.*
> ~ *The Book of Changes (I Ching)*

Families work this way, so do the world and society. The action of abortion is accumulating evil, and the nation that accumulates evil is sure to suffer abundant misery. Of course, the world that accumulates evil is also sure to befall numerous catastrophes.

To resolve this problem, we must advocate sage education.

Sage education can solve the problem from its fundamental root.

I was encouraged by our Dharma teacher Master Chin Kung to give a course about "The Virtues Adolescents Should Have." During this course, I talked about filial piety and the precept of "no sexual misconduct." The origin of some social problems, its root cause, is the excessive lust among young people. Because young people today do not know self-discipline, they create endless karmic sins. This problem is so serious. Please forgive me for emphasizing it.

The Same Mother for Many Lives

Let's return to the main topic, Catherine. While talking under hypnosis, she said that she entered her mother's womb and soon she was born. She felt she was held up by someone, possibly the nurse who delivered her. Then her mother sat next to her, and she was the same mother she had in this life.

It seems that the same soul had been her mother for many lives. So we must understand that the aspiration of our parents' love and care for us lasts more than one lifetime. Catherine's mother in a remembered life is still her mother in this life. As children, we should be grateful to our parents for the immense debt of gratitude that they bestow upon us.

Life as a Male German Air Force Pilot

Catherine told her doctor that in another reincarnation, she became a male pilot in the German Air Force during World War II. In reincarnation, we are sometimes male and sometimes female. There is no certain gender. When starting to learn Buddhism, people often ask,

> *Is Avalokiteśvara Bodhisattva**
> *male or female?*

Just look at our own reincarnation. Sometimes we are male, sometimes female—then why can't Avalokiteśvara Bodhisattva manifest as either male or female?

Catherine said her name during the World War II incarnation was Erik. At that time, their army invaded France and he was stationed in a city in France named Alsace. The pilot had a wife and a daughter. Their life was blessed and they were a happy family. His daughter in that life, Catherine said, is now one of her good friends in this life. Her name is Judy.

There seems to have been some tacit understanding between Judy and Catherine. When they first met, it was like déjà vu. They felt like old friends at first glance. They felt cordial and affectionate with each other, and they always had a sense of telepathy. They understood each other's needs without words. No wonder! They had been father and daughter in the past life.

Many people do not want to learn Buddhism too early, because they still want to enjoy their happiness now. Yet happiness does not last long. Life is impermanent!

---

*Avalokiteśvara Bodhisattva, one of The Three Saints in Sukhavāti, is the Bodhisattva of Compassion and is depicted as either male or female. The Three Saints of Sukhavāti are Amitabha, Avalokiteśvara Bodhisattva, and Mahāsthāmaprāpta Bodhisattva. A bodhisattva is someone who aspires to Supreme Enlightenment and Buddhahood for themselves and all beings.

Erik's happiness did not last long. At a German military party where everyone was happily singing, dancing, and drinking, suddenly the British-American allied forces' aircraft came. The British-American allies were fighting with them in France at that time. The aircraft bombed this German base. In seconds, the party became an ocean of fire.

At that moment, Catherine, in her hypnotic state, saw a sea of flames surround her. Many people were burned to death or killed by the bombs' explosions. Erik sustained serious injuries to his chest and legs and was bleeding heavily. As she described this, Catherine's expression was nervous and distressed. Erik had obviously died in excruciating pain. After a while, under the doctor's guidance, Catherine slowly recovered and restored her calmness.

Many Lives, Many Masters

Catherine said that her soul drifted out of Erik's body, and she was waiting for some people. The doctor, who was recording the session, asked her, "Who are you waiting for? Please speak out." She said, "I am waiting for some gods to come."

Let me insert an explanation here. This patient often reported seeing gods when she was under hypnosis and experiencing a transition from one life to another. These gods could sometimes convey messages to Dr. Weiss through Catherine.

There are questions and there will be answers.

The gods' voice was not the voice of the patient herself. It was very resounding and powerful, a very dignified voice. It sounded like the voice of gods. Dr. Weiss called these gods "masters." His book is titled *Many Lives, Many Masters*, yet the translated Chinese version is titled *Last and Present Life*. Actually, if we translate the American title directly, it would be "Many Reincarnation Lives, Many Spiritual Masters." *Last and Present Life* is a paraphrased translation. Dr. Weiss recorded the voice of these gods and wrote a later book based on these recordings.

Gods Affirm Regression Therapy

The words from these gods are very wise and filled with philosophy. Their information definitely did not come from Catherine, who was a simple-minded person with psychological disorders. Let me give you some examples. The messages from these gods were playing the same tune as Buddha Dharma on different instruments.

It began with such a voice, a very resounding and powerful voice, coming through this female patient's mouth. It sounded similar to a spiritual possession. The voice said, "You use this method to guide patients into a stable state believing it can cure their psychological illness; you are correct. It can help patients to eliminate their inner fear and anxiety. Fear and anxiety are only the superficial symptoms of their problems. You can only help them enter their own deep consciousness to resolve their own problems. The existence of the physical body is an abnormal phenomenon."

This is very similar to what Laozi said: "My biggest worry is that I have this body."

The god continued, "A normal life is a spiritual life. We feel pain in our flesh, but we do not feel pain in the state of spirit, only happiness. The spirit life exists in a different dimension where they continuously work on self-innovation and self-perfection." These were also among the revelations from the gods:

Messages from the Gods

> *Life is endless,*
> *people will never die,*
> *nor are they actually born.*

This revelation indicates that the gods in Catherine's hypnotic trances were in a very high realm, where there is neither birth nor death.

> *We exist only in different forms of flesh and space,*
> *never ceasing.*
> *The reason why people come to this world*
> *in the form of physical existence*
> *is either to complete missions or to return debt.*

This is similar to what the Buddha Dharma stated. People who came to this world are here to "return debt of gratitude or seek revenge, collect debt or repay debt." If you are not here for reasons above, then you are here for a mission. But what mission is it?

Everyone, by chanting Amitabha here, will be able to protect and uphold the Proper-Dharma, and will be able to maintain the saints' and sages' teachings as well. This is called "coming to the world for a mission." This is the merit of saints and the great vocation of sages. If you are not in this vocation, then you are here to repay your debt. The Buddha told us, "Life is simply to receive our karmic retribution."

Your encounter with your next life will be entirely created by yourself.

What Goes Around Comes Around

This god gave us a straightforward revelation of "What goes around comes around." Whatever karma you create in this life will cause retribution in your next life or beyond. Buddha Dharma states,

> *If you want to know your past life,*
> *look into your present conditions.*
> *If you want to know your future life,*
> *look into your present actions.*

This means that whatever the conditions of your present life are, they are all caused by the deeds of your past lives. Look! These gods also revealed the same messages as the Buddha Dharma revealed to us!

We must know, life is just a changing of our physical forms—our bodies. And it happens constantly. We simply come to receive our karmic retribution. We come to repay our debts. If we do not understand this *truth*, we might give rise to bad thoughts and create bad karma while receiving retribution, which will lead us to receive more retribution of suffering in our future.

We create karma due to our delusion, and we suffer from retribution due to the karma we created. The cycle of "being deluded, making karma, and receiving retribution" is endless. Being reincarnated life after life, we continue to sink into the depravity of the wheel of "delusion, karma, and suffering." It is truly dreadful.

Each One of Us Are Equal, Are the Same

The following revelation by the gods is also brilliant: "Each one of us are equal, are the same."

When the god spoke this sentence, Dr. Weiss interrupted the god's revelation. Using Catherine, his female patient, as the medium, he began a dialogue with the god. The doctor asked, "Each of us are different from the perspective of appearance, physique, fortune, wealth, job, talent, and so forth, how can you say that each of us are the same, are no different?"

At this time, the god answered with a metaphor. This godly voice said, "Diamonds are glittering and colorful, yet their shine will be concealed if there is grime on its surface. The inequality in our appearance is just like the thick or thin grime of the diamond that makes us manifest differently. But our true heart is always like the diamond, glittering and colorful, with no difference at all."

Aha, this doctor became enlightened from these words!

He understood the *truth*!

In fact, the revelation from this god and the Buddha Dharma's teaching are like different tunes played with equal skills. You see, after Shakyamuni Buddha became enlightened and achieved His Buddhahood, sitting under the Bodhi tree, the first statement He spoke was,

> *What a wonder! What a wonder!*
> *All sentient beings have the same wisdom, virtues,*
> *and laksana as Tathagata (One of ten titles of a Buddha),*
> *but they could not realize and attain them*
> *due to the delusion and attachment.*

This is very similar to the revelation that this god spoke to Dr. Weiss. Every individual being, including each of us, has all the wisdom, virtues, and laksana (Skt., referring to form, external appearance, or a distinctive feature) of Tathagata, which means that we are the same as Buddhas.

We are equal to, and no different from, Buddhas!

Our Buddha Nature Is Simply Shrouded

But why do we not emit the glittering, colorful light like Tathagata? The Buddha told us it is because of our delusion and attachment. These delusions and attachments are like the grime on the diamond. Our grime is very thick; we are deeply lost, so our wisdom, virtues, and laksana of Tathagata are completely concealed.

Among the six realms of reincarnation, the highest realm is heaven and the lowest realm is hell; this can be attributed to the different thickness of the grime. The thicker the grime, the more deluded one will be. The grime of the hell beings is the thickest, so they are the most deluded. The lighter the grime, the less deluded one will be. For those in our human realm and heaven realm, the grime is thinner.

Every sentient being is the same—but for some of us, delusion leads to the loss of our self-nature, the loss of the diamond of our self-nature; so our glimmering, colorful diamond cannot shine. Actually, it does still shine, but the sparkle is concealed by the grime. As soon as we renounce our defilements, the diamond can shine its colorful glimmer, and it is no different from all Buddhas'! The key to enlightenment, then, is to remove the grime of our delusions and attachments.

Dr. Weiss' book *Messages from the Masters* became a bestseller and has been translated into many different languages.

Through his medical discoveries, Dr. Weiss transformed completely. He changed from having a traditional scientific mind—a doctoral mind trained at Yale University—to totally believing in reincarnation.

Affirmed by Fellow Psychiatrists for His Research

When his book *Many Lives, Many Masters* was completed, Dr. Weiss hesitated to publish it. Why? Because although he had seen many instances where patients appeared to remember their past lives, no scientific research had proved reincarnation at that time.

It was the 1980s, and such studies were relatively scarce. Dr. Weiss was already a well-known scholar and held a certain position in academic circles. He was afraid that it would affect his career if he published this book which contradicted traditional scientific concepts. It was not easy for him to decide! However, based on his scientific attitude of seeking the truth through serious and actual experiences, he decided to proceed.

This scientist is really remarkable. In the end, he devoted himself spiritually to science, encouraged by the spirit of sixteenth century Italian astronomer and physicist Galileo Galilei. To his surprise, after his book was published, his career was not diminished and his fame grew greater. *Many Lives, Many Masters* ranked as the top-selling book for two consecutive years in the United States. It has been translated into eleven languages and is popular all around the world.

Dr. Weiss also received letters from many readers and from his peers. When he received letters from professionals in his own field, his heart was trembling, "Would they criticize me, saying I am anti-science?" To his amazement, these professional psychiatrists not only congratulated him on his book publication but told him they had made similar scientific discoveries, which they did not dare to release. They were happy to find out that someone else has written about reincarnation, and they congratulated him. Dr. Weiss has since become known as the scientific authority in the field of reincarnation.

ALAN LEE, AN EGYPTIAN PHARAOH
IN A FORMER LIFE

Dr. Weiss is the most famous, but not the only medical doctor who has used hypnosis to study reincarnation. American psychiatrist Dr. Irving Mordes reported on a case so extraordinarily splendid that I simply must introduce it to you. A patient of Dr. Mordes, an American man named Alan Lee, was able to recall sixteen past lives while under the doctor's hypnosis. He entered into a deep, tranquil state under the doctor's guidance. Within this dhyana-like state, he recalled not only details of his past lives, but he could also even

> *speak the language of that life and*
> *write the characters of that language.*

Alan Lee, a Philadelphia native, was thirty-eight when he underwent hypnosis for the first time. As a poor academic student, he had dropped out before graduating from middle school. Afterward, he worked a little in different fields. A cancer diagnosis prompted him to accept Dr. Mordes' offer of hypnotherapy.

During his hypnosis, he recalled that, in one of his lives, he had been an Egyptian pharaoh, a king of Egypt. His name was Kallikrates, and he ruled Egypt for only four years,

doctor was always falling behind in her expenses. She seemed to never have enough money to spend. Where did her money go? She squandered all of her income on horses. She could not stop buying horses and decorations for them. She felt very troubled and asked Dr. Beauregard to perform hypnosis on her.

Under hypnosis, she saw that in her past life, she had been a racehorse in the '20s, racing in various southern states in the United States. Her name was Zenyatta, and she became a famous racer.

In other cases, people under hypnosis have remembered being reincarnated as big grizzly bears, and one man said he had been a python. As he recalled his past life during hypnosis, he said that one day the python took a sunbath in a ravine when a volcano suddenly erupted and the lava buried him alive. There were also people who had become rattlesnakes, panthers, and so on.

From the cases above, we can see that some habits of ours and the relationships between people and sentient beings around us are determined by past lives. Hypnosis has been a tool that psychologists and other researchers have used to find evidence of reincarnation by helping patients to recall their past lives, and further, to treat their disorders. It is acknowledged as having rendered a significant effect.

AREA FOUR:
STUDIES OF LIFE
IN DIFFERENT DIMENSIONS

The fourth area of reincarnation research involves the study of life in different dimensions. These might include ghosts, deities, and heavenly beings, or angels as they are called by Westerners. Those lives that cannot be seen by our naked eyes can all be classified as the lives of different dimensions. Science has developed methods to communicate with these beings.

TALKING WITH SPIRITS BY RADIO
—PROOF VIA SOUND

A well-known Italian expert in this area, Dr. Marcello Bacci, began quite early in 1949 to use radio equipment to study the lives of those beings in different dimensions. Through decades of research, he found that by using an electron tube of radio equipment, he was able to hear and perfectly record the messages of these spirits. In some instances, he recorded entire conversations between the researchers and beings in the spirit realm.

Bacci's researchers were generally people who specialized in psychiatry and supernatural science and experts who communicate with beings in different dimensions. Besides them there also were experts in the field of radio and electronic equipment. Sometimes, Bacci's laboratory would have up to seventy people in it. In addition to these experts, Bacci's experiments attracted people who wished to communicate with the dead, including mothers of children who had died. These women were considered prime research subjects because they often had the best success in communicating with those spirits.

The experiments were typically conducted from seven to nine p.m. Bacci chose evening because the spirits are most active at night. For example, *The Zhong Feng Thrice Yearning*

Ceremony*, which many of you have participated in, is held in the afternoon and evening. The reason is to summon the spirits and demonstrate a good example for them, so as to help them become liberated.

Dr. Bacci usually set the radio equipment to seven to nine megahertz. In this frequency band, the laboratory could ensure no interference from any other electromagnetic signals like broadcasts, television, or mobile phones. Some normal static noise would appear initially, but after ten to twenty minutes, the static noise would disappear and would be followed by the sound of a gust of wind, as if the spirit had come with the wind.

And then Dr. Bacci would immediately call out with the radio, "My friends, we are here, where are you? Please speak." After a while, he would hear a reply from the radio speaker: "I am coming." As if they were guests who had arrived, the voices would then start to speak. Often, it was not a single spirit's voice but many voices. They started to talk to the people in the laboratory. Many of them were deceased children who came back to talk to their mothers. Each dialogue usually lasted three to four minutes. After the dialogue finished, the speaker would sound out a burst of singing, as if they sang a song and left. The radio speaker returned to its original static noise, and the experiment was over.

---

*The Thrice Yearning Ceremony is based on *The Amitabha Sutra* to recite the Buddha's name of Amitabha. "Thrice" refers to reciting *The Amitabha Sutra* three times and yearning for Amitabha and His Pure Land to keep a continuous and uninterrupted pure mind.

The dialogue could be heard very genuinely and was also recorded. In one recording, a voice said, "Dear mother!" Obviously he was speaking to one of the mothers who participated in the laboratory. That spirit's name was Gregorio, an Italian name. The deceased child said to his mother, "Dear mother, don't be sad." He comforted her. "One day you will eventually know our mystery. When you leave the body, you will find out that your soul has entered a different level of life."

There were many more dialogues like this, which indicate that the voices were not static noise or other signals. Dr. Bacci conducted these experiments for decades, collecting an abundant amount of data.

The Most Sensational Experiment

Dr. Bacci's most successful experiment was conducted on the evening of December 5, 2004 in his Italian laboratory.

The experts who participated with Dr. Bacci came from Britain, Italy, and Portugal. These were well-known researchers who study supernatural phenomena. In this experiment, when they received the dialogue of these spiritual beings, they removed the recording device's electron tube—the tube that can receive the signals. This means if there were any radio signals, it would be impossible for them to be picked up. Yet Dr. Bacci's device still emanated the dialogue of the spirits as usual. This indicates that the sounds from beings in different dimensions do not rely on our technology. The dialogue was still recorded.

Afterward, more than thirty of the most famous senior professors published a joint report on this experiment. It created quite a stir by seeming to prove that there are indeed lives who exist in other dimensional spaces. But it begs the question:

> *Why are those beings who live in different dimensions able to come when we summon them?*

Summoning Deceased Spirits with Our Thoughts

Now that we have learned about Dharma, in fact, it should be easier to understand this. At the time we are calling these spirits, our mind is thinking of them, and the mind has a great power of attraction. The mind can compel these sentient beings to come over. When we are performing the ritual according to *The Zhong Feng Thrice Yearning Ceremony* or other religious rituals, the first thing we do is invite those deceased souls to come so they can dignify themselves in this solemn rite.

The summoning is very important—and when you think of deceased spirits, the power of your mind can call them over.

Now we know that even an ordinary sentient being can be drawn over, what if we are thinking of Amitabha? Amitabha has never stopped thinking of us—as *Mahasthamaprapta Bodhisattva's Preaching on Being Mindful of the Buddha* states,

> *The way of Amitabha thinking of us is like a mother mindful of her children.*

Amitabha thinks of all beings with every thought, as if a mother missing her children; if we sentient beings think of Amitabha and recite His name, if we ask Amitabha to come to escort us, He will absolutely come. The compelling power of the mind is inconceivable! As such, Mahasthamaprapta Bodhisattva said,

> *If sentient beings*
> *are mindful of Amitabha*
> *and recite His name,*
> *they will certainly see Amitabha*
> *at the present time*
> *or in the future.*

It will be certain that they will see Amitabha. This saying is extremely affirmative.

Many Scholars Have Studied Spiritual Life

Many scholars, in addition to Dr. Bacci, have studied spiritual life. Some of the more famous ones include:

1). Dr. David Fontana of the U.K., a professor of psychology at John Moores University in Liverpool, whose masterwork is about the study of spiritual life after death: *Is There an Afterlife? A Comprehensive Overview of the Evidence* (2005).

2). Dr. Ernst Senkowski of Germany, a physics professor at the University of Mainz of Science & Technology, whose masterwork is:
Instrumental Transcommunication.

3). Dr. Felice Masi of Italy, the president of the Italian Spiritual Study Society, who is an expert in this field as well.

Some might ask, "Since science has developed the use of radio equipment to hear beings in different dimensions, can we also take pictures of beings in different dimensions?" This is, of course, more difficult than capturing their voices—but it is possible.

A GHASTLY SURPRISE IN A GRAVEYARD
—PROOF VIA IMAGE

In February of 2004, an Indian scholar visited an indigenous tribe on a forest reservation in India. This scholar planned to live with the tribe in order to understand better how they lived harmoniously with nature. The Indian scholar met a Japanese anthropology graduate student who also planned to visit this tribe to gather information for his thesis. They went together and stayed peacefully with the tribe for several days.

The ancestors of this tribe live in a sacred graveyard where outsiders are not allowed to enter. But these two scholars did not know this. One day, while walking in the forest reservation, they accidentally entered the graveyard where the souls of this tribe's ancestors live. It was dusk at that time. The Indian scholar took a photo of the Japanese student with a digital camera—but almost immediately, the Japanese student suddenly fell to the ground, unconscious. The worried Indian scholar rushed to ask the tribal elders for help. They hurried to the scene, suspecting this was the doing of their ancestors. The tribal elders must have encountered this many times before. They seemed very experienced. They chanted a mantra and then gave the fallen student some herbal medicine, and he recovered quickly.

Later, back at his own university, the Indian scholar began to download his photos from the trip to his computer. When he downloaded the picture he took at dusk, he broke out in a cold sweat. This picture clearly showed a spirit standing behind the Japanese student.

Of course, we can speculate that this spirit was the soul of the tribal ancestor. The student offended them, so one stood behind him and maybe also gave him a kick or hit and made him faint. Do not look for long at this photo, because it might cause you to lose sleep tonight.

98 Percent of the Universe Is Invisible to Our Naked Eyes

The digital camera, which can capture images that are unseen by our human eyes, has certain scientific applications. We know that the human eye can only detect 2 percent of the optical spectrum. We call this 2 percent "visible light"—lights with longer wavelengths like electromagnetic waves and infrared rays, and lights with shorter wavelengths such as ultraviolet and gamma rays—they cannot be seen by the naked human eye. In other words, humans can see only 2 percent of the entire universe with their eyes, while

98 percent of the universe is invisible to us. Since the photosensitivity of the camera is broader than the sensitivity of the human eye, the image of different dimensions can be captured on film even if an object cannot be seen by human eyes.

We know that X-rays can damage the photosensitivity of film negatives. If we put a film under an X-ray, the film can no longer record photos. Even though human eyes cannot see X-rays due to their shorter wavelength, we can see the effect of an X-ray; this proves the existence of X-rays. Digital cameras now use a photoreceptor that is a semiconductor, an array called a CCD. Each photosensitive particle, we call a pixel. There are cameras with five million pixels or seven million pixels. The higher the pixel count, the more clear the image, because it has more photosensitive particles. A digital camera can capture an even broader spectrum than film negatives can; it is used widely even in astronomical telescopes to photograph the rays of many other galaxies.

So the Indian scholar was able to capture the image of a spirit at dusk, a spirit unseen by human eyes. His high-pixel camera could capture this image because of technology that can be explained by scientific principles. Of course, there is not a great deal of research in this area, and we are still waiting for science to further develop and confirm our theories.

This fourth area of our discussion proves that reincarnation may also exist in many different forms of life, including in the form of a ghost or spirit. It is stated in Buddhism that we exist in an intermediate state for forty-nine days after death. During this period of time, the soul exists as a different form of life for a short term.

THE STUDY OF
SUPERNATURAL POWER

In some Western countries, especially the United States, there are people recognized as having supernatural power. They are called "psychics." Some of them have made great contributions to scientific research about reincarnation. Some even had a great influence on mainstream scientific research because their supernatural power can cure unknown and complicated diseases that cannot be cured by general medical methods. Some of them are even able to see the past and predict the future.

THE CASES OF
MIRACLE WORKER CAYCE

One such psychic was Edgar Cayce, who was born in 1877 and died in 1945. He was able to go into a hypnotic trance without assistance; sometimes, during these trances, spirits would enter his body and give medical advice or predictions. Cayce often said that the patients' illnesses in their current lives were caused by events in their past lives. Cayce believed the root cause of illness involved reincarnation.

Cayce had a high profile because of his success in curing patients. A mother in Kentucky whose baby was born with a seizure disorder once contacted Cayce for help. Three specialists were giving her child treatments, but he was getting worse and doctors predicted he would die. Cayce received guidance during a trance advising the mother to give the baby a poisonous extract from the atropa belladonna plant.

The doctors strongly opposed the idea of giving the child a poisonous drug, but the desperate mother insisted on following Cayce's advice. Soon after taking the medicine, this little boy slowly recovered and stopped twitching. He fully recovered from the disease shortly after. This was a miracle in the history of medicine! Cayce treated 14,000 cases in his lifetime, many with great success.

His practices came under scrutiny by skeptics who thought he might be setting up a scam, fishing for fortune and fame. Harvard University psychologist Dr. Hugo Münsterberg carefully investigated Cayce. In the end, he and the other skeptics were convinced that Cayce indeed had supernatural power. A special museum in the U.S. was dedicated to him and a foundation continues to do this type of work in his name.

Cayce diagnosed 2,500 cases related to reincarnation, which were the focus of several studies. Gina Cerminara, PhD, wrote a book about her research called *Many Mansions: The Edgar Cayce Story on Reincarnation*.

Cayce sometimes observed the patients' past lives to find the root cause of the illness in this life. He usually called the root cause "karma." His explanation for karma is as follows:

> *Karma is like the weapon that*
> *Australian aboriginal people use,*
> *the boomerang.*
> *When one throws out a boomerang*
> *to strike a flying object, such as a bird,*
> *the boomerang will return to the person*
> *who threw it.*

The cycle of karma is similar to a boomerang's action, he said.

Whatever you do,
the impact of karma
will come back to you.
If you do good deeds,
you will get good rewards;
if you do evil deeds,
you will get evil retribution.

A Real Example of the Karma of Poisoning Others

A forty-year-old woman came to Cayce once for help with her allergies. When she ate food containing grains, she would sneeze constantly. When she encountered leather or things like plastic, she would experience nerve pain throughout her body. Doctors had told her there was no way to cure her disease.

Cayce observed this woman in his self-hypnosis state and pointed out that her disease had its root cause in her past life. He said in one of her lifetimes, she had been a chemist who studied and developed chemical drugs. Many people had allergic reactions to these drugs, especially with some that polluted the air. Her allergies were due to this karma. Cayce instructed her to repent and gave her a prescription, which finally cured her.

Blinding Others Causes Blindness in a Future Life

In another case, a professor who had been blind since birth came to Cayce. Many experts had given her treatment, but to no effect. She was very smart and became a university professor, yet she could see nothing because both her eyes were blind. She had heard of Cayce while listening to a radio program called "Miracle of the Mind," which discussed supernatural topics and claimed Cayce's healing was magical.

Cayce observed the professor's past lives and saw that in 1000 BC, she had lived in Persia, where Iran is today. She had been a member of a barbaric tribe there which tortured and mutilated their enemies, including burning their eyes with a red-hot piece of iron. This professor had blinded many people during that life, so she received the retribution of being born blind.

Cayce also instructed her to repent. Within three months, she was able to acquire 10 percent vision. From this case, we can see the impact of past lives on present-day illnesses. The Buddhist sutras state,

> *If you want to know your past life,*
> *look into your present conditions.*
> *If you want to know your future life,*
> *look into your present actions.*

What goes around will definitely come around. Once we understand the *truth* of reincarnation, we must be vigilant and prevent ourselves from taking the wrong step.

Creating Karma
by Using the Bible to Denounce Others

I've given examples of how "doing evil deeds begets evil retribution," but in fact, we also beget retribution with our evil thoughts. Even if we have not taken any action, we have to pay the price for just having an evil thought. Another of Cayce's cases explains it.

A woman sought Cayce's help for a gynecological disease. Since puberty, her menstruation had been abnormal; every four weeks, she had to lie in bed for two weeks to recover from her monthly cycle. The great amount of bleeding made her feel too ashamed to see people, so she became introverted and withdrawn.

Cayce observed her past lives and finally found the reason.

In one life, this woman had been a Catholic nun in the age of King Louis XIV in France. She was very familiar with the Bible and the religious classics—but regretfully, she did not use that wisdom to regulate herself! She did not cultivate herself, but instead used the classics as the basis to severely criticize the flaws of other people. Whenever someone violated the commandments or did not meet the teachings of the classics, she would rebuke them and make them ashamed to see other people. Because she had made others feel ashamed and afraid to see people by harshly denouncing others' faults, her retribution in this life was being ashamed to see others because of her disease.

Real practitioners, holding the saints' and sages' classics like the Buddhist scriptures, must not use them to regulate others. The sages' classics should be used to regulate ourselves. If we used the classic norms of saints and sages to regulate others, not only would our learning of the classics have no merits, but we would also even create a great sin. The Sixth Patriarch of Zen Buddhism, Master Hui Neng, said,

> *He who treads the path in earnest*
> *sees not the mistakes of the world.*

This means that real practitioners will not see faults in other people, but will use these classics to set standards for himself. If we use our time to improve our own virtues, we won't have the idle time to care about other peoples' business.

The Effect of Blaming Fate
and Everyone Else

In the last of Cayce's cases that I will share today, a thirty-four-year-old patient named Paul Durbin suffered from multiple sclerosis, commonly known as "spinal tuberculosis" in those days. His nerves were affected to the extent that he experienced atrophy in his right leg and hand, and he lost his ability to work.

His wife and children were relying on his income, so he was troubled about being unable to work. His finances were in bad shape. Friends had sympathized with his situation and offered him help, sometimes even paying his medical expenses. But this patient had developed psychological problems, always immersing himself in a resentful mood. He complained about his doctor for not curing his disease. Sometimes he even complained about the people who helped him. This habit of blaming fate and everyone else but himself was quite serious; his heart was full of resentment and injustice, and he would vent it on everyone around him. His attitude made his friends sad. Some even regretted ever helping him.

Cayce gave him a prescription—not medicine, but a mental prescription. Cayce saw that, in one of this patient's past lives, he had excessively immersed himself in negative emotions. His heart was full of selfishness, resentment, and grudges. His negative energy then had caused his disease in this lifetime, and his bad attitude followed him as well. He had not committed any sinful deeds—but his resentful mentality led him to illness. Cayce knew he could not recover unless he corrected his psychologically ill mind.

> *Only by correcting these mental problems,*
> *can one's physical problems get well.*

This is an excerpt from Cayce's prescription:

> *You must get rid of these negative emotions*
> *from your heart,*
> *everything has its retribution,*
> *precise to a hair's breadth.*
> *This disease, the nerve atrophy disease,*
> *is caused by karma.*
> *As long as there is*
> *hatred, viciousness, and selfish thoughts,*
> *the disease will not be cured.*
> *To change the physical condition,*
> *you should first change your mind.*
> *You must take measures to change your attitude*
> *towards the environment, the objects, and your colleagues.*
> *Any treatment would not lead to a complete recovery,*
> *you will have hope only if you purify your soul.*

This was the mental prescription that Cayce gave him: to purify his soul; because his illness had been caused by the evil thoughts entangled in his heart and by his selfishness, complaining about fate, and blaming everyone else.

Even After Kalpas,
Our Karma Will Not Vanish

A mental illness requires the cure from one's own heart. Cayce had him purify his soul, repent the evil thoughts in his past, and eliminate these evil thoughts completely from his heart. Only then was it possible for him to restore his health. The Buddhist sutras have a statement,

> *Even after hundreds of thousands of kalpas,*
> *our karma would not vanish,*
> *When the causes and conditions meet together,*
> *the retribution will still be received.*

This means that even after hundreds of thousands of kalpas—an inconceivably long time—the karma you have created will never disappear. When the causes and conditions are all in place, the retribution will manifest, and you will receive the retribution. Even if there was only one evil thought in your life, that evil thought will still lead to retribution in the future. It goes without saying that if you commit bad deeds, their retribution can absolutely not be escaped.

CHAPTER FOUR

REVEALING THE ORIGINS OF REINCARNATION—Avarice, Resentment, Attachment, and More

N ow we know that people experience reincarnation and are implicated and dominated by cause and effect. But,

How do people come to reincarnation?
What is the cause?

Let's explore the origins of reincarnation with some scientific examples. Dr. Bryan Jameison, a well-known expert of reincarnation studies in the U.S., began his research into past lives and healing in the late 1960s. He invented a so-called "non-regression hypnotic method," which helped patients return to their past lives within a few minutes.

Dr. Jameison accumulated more than forty years of research experience and published many books, including *The Search for Past Lives: Exploring the Reincarnation Mysteries and The Amazing Healing Power of Past Life Therapy.*

A few cases from this book shed light on the origin of reincarnation.

DEPRESSION FROM A LIFE
DURING WORLD WAR II

A girl named Nancy suffered from psychological depression from a young age. She always felt guilt and shame. Although she had a happy family, she could not control her sense of guilt. She felt that it was shameful to live in the world, so she attempted suicide three times, but she was rescued every time.

Dr. Jameison helped her to recall her past lives. In one of them, she had been a sixteen-year-old girl in Europe during World War II. Her family lived happily together until, one day when they were eating dinner, Hitler's fascist army suddenly broke into their house and arrested them. Her father protested, saying, "You cannot arrest people like this." The Nazis shot him on the spot. She and her mother, as well as her brother, were dragged down the stairs. Her brother attempted to pull away and run down the street, but he was also shot and fell dead to the ground.

When she saw this tragic scene—a happy family destroyed by this fascist army in seconds—she reported feeling very sad. She felt the sky and Earth were spinning, and then she got very dizzy and passed out. She woke up in a truck with many other people who had also been arrested, encountering misfortune like her. Then, they were packed into a crowded train, like sardines. They had to do everything on the train—eating, drinking, defecating, and urinating—just like animals, with no respect or dignity at all.

When the train arrived at a station, they were pushed into a concentration camp like livestock. Their hair was cut and they were given prisoner uniforms. Then they were enslaved. She and another girl were selected to serve those fascist officers as sex objects. This girl played piano very well and was liked by a Nazi officer, who presented a bouquet to her to show his affection. Later, when this Nazi officer pursued pleasure with her, she even had a delusion, thinking she might live with this young officer forever after the war ended.

The Horrific Anguish of Guilt

One day, this Nazi officer brought her to a yard where a crowd of people were walking. She asked the young officer, "Where are these people heading to?" That officer smiled and said that they were going to enter the gas chamber, which meant that they were going to be killed. At that moment, one person in the crowd turned around and she recognized her mother. She was following this group of people who were about to enter the gas chamber.

The day after this incident, this girl felt overwhelmed by guilt. Her heart was full of anguish. Her entire family had been killed by the monsters of this fascist army, yet she was still here pursuing pleasure with an enemy officer; she even had a fantasy of living with him later. She ended her own life by slashing her wrist. However,

> *The sense of guilt in her heart*
> *did not die with her death*
> *but followed her soul*
> *and reincarnated to this life.*

As a consequence, she felt an extremely deep sense of guilt since her childhood and often had the thought of committing suicide in this life. This karma… what do we see from it? Chinese ancients said,

> *Better to die in glory than live in disgrace.*

It might be better to sacrifice one's life than drag out an existence with demons. Wen Tianxian* said in one of his poems,

> *Since time began,*
> *to die who can decline?*
> *Through history books in glory,*
> *let our crimson hearts shine!*

As humans, we should live in a dignified and upright manner. We should not live with demons; otherwise, this guilt, this feeling of deficit to the soul, will not be obliterated for life after life.

A FEAR OF BIRDS:
A TRAGIC RETRIBUTION FOR RAPE

Dr. Jameison also treated an American patient named Barbara who had an inexplicable fear of birds. Most of us like birds. Why would someone be afraid of them?

When Barbara was twenty-seven years old, she took a walk on the beach with a friend one day. Her friend took some popcorn to feed the seagulls. When the seagulls swooped down to fight over the food, one seagull swept its wings over Barbara's face. That moment triggered an inexplicable fear in Barbara. From that day on, she was terrified of birds. Before leaving the house, she always looked out the window to see if any birds

---

*Wen Tianxian, 1236-1283, was a famous poet in The Southern Song Dynasty. He left masterpieces like *The Song of the Righteous Spirit* and *Crossing the Lonely Ocean*, which have influenced Chinese people for nearly 1,000 years.

were nearby. If she saw birds, she would not dare to go out. She always brought an umbrella when she walked in the street, because she was afraid that a bird would swoop down to attack her. This had become a psychological condition, and eventually, she asked for Dr. Jamison's help.

Under hypnosis, she recalled one of her past lives at the end of the 19th century. She had lived in the Southwestern U.S. and was a white male. When this man was twenty-seven years old, he got drunk and raped a Native American girl. When one has idle time, they will usually do bad things after drinking. The Confucian classic *Mencius* has a saying,

> *There are principles to be learned*
> *for being a human.*
> *If one is fed well, clad warmly,*
> *and lodged comfortably,*
> *yet not educated by the principles,*
> *he will become almost like a beast.*

In other words, if you have nothing to do after eating contently, and if you do not try learning sage teachings, you might act out the deeds of beasts. Then your retribution would certainly be tragic.

The Native American family of this man's victim was so angry, they sent warriors to kidnap him. The warriors dragged him to the desert, ripped off his clothes, and then tied his hands behind his back. Before they left, one of the warriors took a knife, carving a wound in his chest. As the blood poured out, the Native American warriors departed and left him alone in that arid desert.

The sun was very strong. It was hot and dry. He was bleeding profusely and quickly collapsed. At this time, he saw a few vultures in the sky circling overhead; they probably smelled the blood. One of the vultures swooped down. He screamed, but the vultures quickly realized he had no ability to defend himself. A few vultures soon rushed forward to fight over and eat his flesh. He experienced such desperate fear, he was literally scared to death. That year, he was the same age as when this female patient, Barbara, suddenly developed her fear of birds. So doing evil deeds will certainly receive evil retribution. The ancients said,

> *Filial piety is the foremost of all virtues,*
> *while sexual misconduct is the top among all evils.*

People who commit sexual misconduct would not be tolerated by heaven and earth; they would enrage all gods and people. The white man who committed this evil deed received his retribution right away—but this retribution left a deep imprint in his heart. Life after life, he carried the shadow of this misery. Buddhist sutras state,

> *Repent from our inner heart, for sins arise from our heart.*
> *When the delusion of our heart is extinguished,*
> *our sins will then be eradicated.*

If you extinguish evil thoughts from your heart, your sins will also vanish. No matter how bad your deeds were, do not carry them with you all of the time; let them go and never do them again.

> *Only when both our delusion and sin are extinguished,*
> *and our heart returns to the emptiness (self-nature, thusness),*
> *it can then be called a "real repentance."*

REVENGE OF THE UNFILIAL HIPPIES
AND ITS SOLUTION

Many of Dr. Jameison's cases clearly illustrate the issue of cause and effect. In the '70s in the United States, a group of hippies who were curious about their past lives visited Dr. Jameison for help. Dr. Jameison found out that most of these hippies were reincarnated from Native Americans. In those lifetimes, these Native Americans had fought a war with white men who were new immigrants to the U.S.

We know that the white man in the United States almost completely annihilated the Native Americans. Those Native Americans who were killed by these white men were reincarnated as white people, often as the children of the white men who had killed them. These Native Americans reincarnated to seek revenge, so they were mostly unfilial at home; this disturbed the social order in the society of white people. Through Dr. Jameison's study, we can see that the causal retribution indeed exists.

Nowadays, often in families, father and son do not get along. When parents and children do not have harmony, it is often related to their past lives. In addition, when something breaches the peace in society—for example, when terrorists attack—their motivation is often from resentment incurred in past lives. This life, they came for revenge!

These resentments must be resolved; if not, the accumulated resentment would become deeper and deeper. As ancients said, "The hostility should be resolved rather than entwined"! We should not use force to oppress, persecute, or kill terrorists. We should resolve their hatred. What about those hippies who reincarnated for revenge—how would their resentment be resolved? Our mentor, Master Chin Kung, told us,

> *To resolve the resentment of the world,*
> *we can only rely on sage education.*

Sage education is indeed the education of gratitude and love. With sincerity, with a grateful attitude and a genuine loving heart, we can resolve the resentment of others.

Only Sage Education Can Resolve the Resentment of the World

Even if resentment is deeply rooted, life after life, it can be resolved when we use our sincere hearts and patience to persistently treat them—we must not be afraid to sacrifice. The only problem is whether we have sincerity or not.

If a soul came for revenge as your child, how could you teach them?

> *You must teach them from childhood.*
> *Sage education must be instilled from their childhood.*

Using the education of *Dizigui (Guidelines for Being a Good Person)* can help save one from the root. What is the root? First of all, as stated in *Dizigui* we must teach them filial piety.

> *The guidelines for being a good person*
> *are exhorted by ancient sages.*
> *And being filial and fraternal is the foremost rule.*

This means we must first teach children filial piety and fraternal love.

When we look at these cases, the parents indeed killed those people in the past—yet the debt of gratitude of giving birth to them and raising them is immeasurable. *The Book of Odes (Shi Jing)* says,

> *Alas! Alas! My parents!*
> *With what a toil you gave me birth!*
> *The debt of gratitude I shall repay*
> *is like great heaven, boundless.*

The deep kindness that our parents bestow upon us is as boundless as the sky. Shakyamuni Buddha elaborated on parents' profound kindness to his disciples in *The Sutra of Unrepayable Grace of Parents*. This sutra gave us a very detailed description of the debt of gratitude that parents—particularly mothers—bestow to their children.

A mother carries a fetus for nearly ten months, enduring any hardship in order to give birth to a healthy baby. After the baby is born, she takes painstaking efforts, both physically and mentally, to ensure her baby grows to be healthy. Loving parents have their every thought for their children. This debt is impossible for children to pay back. The Buddha gave us an analogy:

> *Even if someone carries their parents*
> *till their bones are broken*
> *and their bone marrow seeps out*
> *for hundreds of thousands of kalpas,*
> *they are still unable to pay back*
> *the debt of gratitude of their parents.*

Even Donating One's Own Kidney
Can Still Not Pay Back the Debt

In February of 2005, there was a program on Chinese Central Television called "The People Who Moved China." The producers had selected ten people who had moved the hearts of China. One of them was a loving child whose filial piety had moved all Chinese people.

Tian Shiguo was a thirty-eight-year-old lawyer in Guangzhou, where I come from. His mother suffered from kidney disease and uremia. The doctor suggested that the best way to treat the disease was to transplant a kidney, but his family was unable to afford a kidney. Tian Shiguo was determined to donate one of his kidneys to his mother without her knowledge. In September 2004, the mother and son had the kidney transplanted successfully in a Shanghai hospital, and both were discharged safely. Even today, the mother does not know that her new kidney was from her son. This filial piety truly touches us.

Yet parents' profound kindness cannot fully be repaid even by making an offering of a kidney. The Buddha stated, even with an offering of bone marrow for hundreds of thousands of kalpas, one still cannot repay their parents' debt of gratitude. Therefore,

> *Even if there were deadly and deep-seated feuds*
> *with our parents in the past,*
> *as children, we should still be filial to them*
> *no matter how grave their faults are.*

Sage Education
Should Start from Filial Piety

Only education can make the children develop a genuine heart of filial piety. Only sage education can resolve the problems and the resentment of past lives. This education is important! As *The Book of Rites* (*Li Ji*) denotes,

> *Education is essential in building a country*
> *and in guiding its people.*

The most important task of a nation is education. We must make sage education the primary mission of a nation. But what should be the priority of education? In other words, what should be taught first? Confucius has already given us an answer. He stated straight to the point in the beginning of *The Classic of Filial Piety*,

> *Filial piety is the root of all virtues,*
> *and it is where all virtue education originates.*

If filial piety is the foundation of all virtues, then all sage education should start from filial piety!

GRUESOME RESPONSE AND RETRIBUTION
OF A MOTHER AND CHILD

We have asked: How do we get reincarnated? The answer is that reincarnation is mostly prompted by "collecting debt, repaying debt, returning the debt of gratitude, and seeking revenge."

Dr. Roger J. Woolger, a psychologist at Oxford University in the U.K. and an expert in the field of reincarnation, had a patient named Paula. This patient wanted to cure some of her psychological problems, so she asked the doctor to help her recall her past lives with hypnosis. In one of her past lives, she discovered she had been a mother in a primitive tribe. This mother had just given birth to a baby. But the tribe lacked food, everybody was hungry. So this mother took an axe to chop her own baby and served it as food. In that life, she was later eaten by some wild beasts.

In the life immediately following, this mother was born into another primitive tribe. This tribe encountered the same problem of starvation, and the mother also killed her baby. During the hypnosis, she saw that this time, she was the baby. The mother who killed her was the baby she had killed in her previous life. To make it clear: The mother killed her own baby in the previous life, and the baby reincarnated to become her mother and killed her in the next life. The causal retribution is truly like the *Treatise on Response and Retribution* states,

> *The retributions of good and evil*
> *are like the shadow following its form.*

REMEMBERING BEING SPEARED TO DEATH BY ONE'S GREAT UNCLE

Allow me to introduce you briefly to two more cases. Professor Stevenson—the famous professor of the University of Virginia in the U.S., had a patient named Charles Porter, a Native American in Alaska. Porter remembered a previous life in which he was also living in a Native American tribe. During a war between Native American tribes, he was killed when an enemy pierced the right side of his chest with a spear. In this life, he has a big birthmark over his right rib in the shape of a diamond, like the wound caused by the head of a spear.

We have discussed Professor Stevenson's birthmark theory, in which a fatal injury in one life shows up as a birthmark in subsequent lives. But this patient was able to recognize the enemy who killed him. It was a relative—his mother's uncle in this life. This means that his great uncle was still alive, although already very old; he had lived until the person he killed was reincarnated into his family. Since Charles Porter remembered his previous life, we can imagine how he felt when he saw the enemy again, this time as his great uncle.

So, the relationship among people is none other than to "collect debt and return debt," or even "collect life debt and return life debt." The famous Buddhist sutra, *The Surangama Sutra*, states,

> *You owe me life, I return the debt,*
> *per this cause and condition,*
> *hundreds of thousands of kalpas passed,*
> *we are in this birth and death perpetually.*

That means, since you owed me life, I will come back to collect my life-debt. If you owe me a debt, you will also have to pay it back. Life after life, we are reincarnated within the relationships of these entangled debts.

REINCARNATED AS
HUSBAND AND SISTER'S DAUGHTER

Professor Stevenson also had a patient who was a girl in Myanmar named Tintinming. She was born in a city called Pinmana on June 6, 1960. Her father was named Lapi, and her mother was named Sang. Lapi's deceased wife was named Huei, who was the current wife's older sister.

After Lapi's former wife died, her sister dreamed that the departed sister told her: "I am going to follow you." The older sister, Huei, had had a good relationship with her husband when alive. They stuck together as firmly and inseparably as glue. After she died, she appeared in her sister's dream and said, "I am going to follow you"—because only in this way could she still be with her dear husband. About one year later, Sang became the second wife of Lapi. Soon after, she was pregnant.

During the pregnancy, she again dreamed of her late sister. The late sister once again expressed her wish to follow her younger sister. The younger sister told her in the dream, "You are no longer in the same world as us now. And I also married your husband. If you always follow me, I am afraid it is not appropriate." But this late sister said in the dream, "The relationship is no longer the same as before. I am determined to follow you."

Sang gave birth to a daughter named Tintinming in 1960. When she was two years old, she was able to recall and describe her previous life as Lapi's wife. Many pieces of evidence, including a thorough investigation, proved Tintinming was indeed the reincarnation of her father's late wife. Tintinming's affection for her past husband remained. Whenever her parents sat together, Tintinming showed her jealousy by wedging herself in between them. Of course, some children are jealous, but this kind of attitude towards parents is not very common. It indicates that the causal relationship of reincarnation is very intricate. *The Surangama Sutra* actually interprets these intricate causal relationships in a simple way. It is none other than this reason:

> *You love my heart, I enamor your beauty,*
> *per this cause and condition,*
> *through hundreds of thousands of kalpas,*
> *we are entangled together.*

This suggests that men and women, in reincarnation, are tied together, life after life, because of their entangled love. Maybe in one life they are husband and wife, but not in the next life. Yet, because their hearts hold love toward each other, there is a "karmic attraction" between them. They are drawn together, causing them to be reincarnated again and again.

CHAPTER FIVE

HOW TO TRANSCEND
REINCARNATION

We have given strong evidence that there is, in fact, re-incarnation, and that causal relationships dominate reincarnation. In these examples we have mentioned those who killed others received miserable consequences, and those bloody murders caused bitter retributions; it is already so em-bittering to be a human, let alone the three evil paths of hell, ghost, and animal. Do we have any way to transcend the ever-lasting bitterness of birth and death?

Modern science has not advanced enough to study these questions. Scientific research can only go so far! To contemplate further, we still need to rely on Buddhist sutras. Our mentor, Master Chin Kung, said,

It is a pity that scientists nowadays
do not read Buddhist sutras.
If they did,
scientists would have more
profound contemplations,
and science today would be more advanced.

Can people transcend reincarnation?

Buddhism has the answer!

Scientists should also move toward this development. This concept was also endorsed by Albert Einstein, the Father of Modern Physics.

NATURAL AND SPIRITUAL, IN ONE MEANINGFUL UNITY—EINSTEIN

Einstein discovered the theory of relativity, quantum mechanics, and the photoelectric effect. His discoveries laid the foundation for modern science and built a basis for the development for astrophysics. He won the Nobel Prize for his contribution to photoelectric effect theory. In an article called *Religion and Science,* Einstein wrote:

> *The religion of the future*
> *(referring to the religion of the 21st century),*
> *will be a cosmic religion.*
> *It (this religion) should transcend a personal God*
> *and avoid dogmas and theology.*
> *Covering both the natural and spiritual,*
> *it should be based on a religious sense*
> *arising from the experience of all things,*
> *natural and spiritual, in a meaningful unity.*

His words *"in a meaningful unity"* are marvelous. Einstein spoke of the universe as one unity! His last sentence is the most brilliant:

> *Buddhism is the religion described above.*
> *If there is any religion that would be able to*

cope with modern scientific needs,
it would be Buddhism.

Einstein had the wisdom to be the Father of Modern Physics. He had pointed out, decades ago, that future scientific development would have to rely on Buddhism.

So, can people transcend reincarnation?
Only in Buddhism can we find the answer!

To understand why people reincarnate, we must first learn the root cause of reincarnation.

MANIFESTED BY THE HEART

Of course, there can be many reasons to reincarnate. Each of you might have the answer in your heart. Yet the Buddha told us that:

The root cause is because we are deluded,
deluded about the truth of life and the universe.
Due to this delusion, we then create karma,
and due to creating karma we suffer from reincarnation.
This is what is described in sutras as "The wheel of
being deluded, making karma, and receiving retribution."

As a matter of fact, reincarnation can be an endless cycle, like a wheel. The Buddha simply used three words—delusion, karma, and suffering—to expound the root cause of this endless birth and death for us. But we have to ask,

Since the root cause is delusion,
what are we deluded about?

The most fundamental delusions, in Buddhist terminology, are:

- **The delusion of view and cognition:**
  Erroneous views and cognition, which hinder nirvana, preventing one from seeing emptiness and attaining nirvana.
- **The delusion of dust-sand:**
  Mental disturbances of a bodhisattva when dealing with innumerable details like dust and sand to help all beings, which hinder one's bodhisattva path. It is the hindrance to understanding the true nature of all phenomena, so one does not have enough skillful means to lead sentient beings to liberation.
- **The delusion of Avidya:**
  The affliction arising from primal nescience which hinders one from the Middle Way. It is the subtlest affliction that prevents one from fully realizing the ultimate reality.

A deeper discussion of these belongs to the theory of doctrines. But the most basic delusion is: we separate ourselves from the "one meaningful unity of the universe and all things" as Einstein referred to. The truth of the universe is "one unity." All things and all beings are the common thread of one life community. If we are deluded about this point, giving rise to a deluded mind, it is called ignorance (avidya). If we think we are not part of one unity, this is ignorance that leads to attachment and discrimination.

Once we differentiate you from me, we have thoughts of selfishness. We might even harm others to benefit ourselves, creating boundless evil karma. Of course, this evil karma will beget retribution—and that is why we suffer endless reincarnation. So the fundamental delusion is denying that we are "the common thread of one life community."

Where does this community come from?

According to Buddhist sutras, the common thread of one life community is

Merely manifested by our heart.

The universe is one unity, and the one unity is our heart!

Buddhism reveals to us that the universe is manifested by self-nature (true heart, true nature, noumenon, thusness, Buddha nature). Our self-nature manifests the vastness of dharma-realms in one thought, manifesting the universe and all things.

MANIFEST IN A "KSANA*"

You may ask, how long have the universe and all the things in it existed? The Buddha told us the truth: its time is only within one thought. The universe and all things manifest in an instant because the thought of our hearts is constantly changing. Our self-nature creates and recreates the universe instantly, yet manifestation also ceases instantly. When another thought arises, it manifests a new realm, and the whole universe is manifested again.

Think of entering a dark room. We turn on the light and the whole room can be seen clearly. Turn off the light, and the room goes dark again. Our thoughts are just like this, on and off, arising and ceasing—too fast to be detected. It is arising

---

* Ksana is a Sanskrit word for a split second, an extremely short time.

and ceasing in a "ksana." This is the *truth* of the universe and life. The "on and off" is so fast that we cannot detect it, so the Buddha called it "non-arising, non-ceasing." In fact, non-arising, non-ceasing is not without arising and ceasing—but the speed of the arising and ceasing happens so fast—in a "ksana"— that what we see is, essentially, non-arising and non-ceasing.

This is the *truth* of the universe and life!

THE RETURN OF SELF-NATURE

Einstein stated that the universe and all things are merged into one unity. But where does this one unity go? We must know that it goes to our *"one thought."*

> *This "one thought of self-nature"*
> *is the origin of the universe and all things,*
> *which is the "noumenon" of the universe and all things,*
> *they merged into one unity here in our "one thought."*
> *This is called the return of self-nature.*

If we are deluded about this *truth* of the universe and life, we will be subject to delusion, discrimination, and attachment, where we repeatedly create karma and receive retribution. The Buddha understands the *truth* of the universe and life, He is not deluded, so He will not create karma, and of course, He will not receive retribution. Although He no longer creates karma, the Buddha will still demonstrate cause and effect in order to edify and liberate all beings.

So, even the Buddha would not intervene in causality!

Although we have been talking about the *truth* of the universe and life in Buddhism, and each of you might understand it, I am afraid that when you finish reading, you will forget again.

You will have all sorts of wandering thoughts, therefore being deluded, creating karma, and receiving retribution again. Due to our "karmic habits," we sentient beings—even if we comprehend this *truth*—will still find it difficult to transform our minds.

Does that mean that we have no way to transcend reincarnation?

There Are Ways!

TRANSCEND REINCARNATION WITH THE PURE LAND METHOD

Shakyamuni Buddha had great compassion. He knew that we sentient beings would not be able to transform our minds and eradicate our sinful karma, even if we understood it. He thus prescribed a special method for us, which is:

Reciting Amitabha and seeking Sukhāvatī rebirth— to be reborn into The Western Pure Land of Ultimate Bliss.

This method of reciting Amitabha is rather profound in theory. If we do not understand "the essence of self-nature," we will not have a deep comprehension of The Pure Land Method. But due to His mercy, Buddha taught us to simply recite a chant to find liberation!

The Buddha let us cultivate from the root. Our "one thought" is the root. The universe and all things merge into one unity, and this one unity is the noumenon of our "one thought of self-nature." Therefore, we should start to cultivate and discipline our thoughts. But how?

The Buddha let us recite Amitabha—using this "one thought" to replace all sorts of our wandering thoughts! Because the thought of Amitabha is a pure thought. If we can recite the pure thought of Amitabha again and again—Amitabha, Amitabha, Amitabha—our thoughts will be purified. If we recite this Buddha's name incessantly, our minds will be purified before we know it. When our thought is purified and limpid, just like the saying in *The Zhong Feng Thrice Yearning Ceremony,*

> *When reciting Amitabha—*
> *just as the "crystal bead" goes into a turbid water,*
> *sinking little by little and turning the water limpid—*
> *your heart will be purified bit by bit*
> *as your recitation of Amitabha continues incessantly.*

Pure Land of Our Own Heart

Then we ask, what kind of realm will this purified mind manifest? That is The World of Ultimate Bliss, Sukhāvatī. The World of Ultimate Bliss is called Pure Land. Pure Land is manifested merely by our own true heart. It is the pure land of our true heart.

This concept is extremely profound. If you understand it, that is great—but if not, no matter. Why? Because if you just recite Amitabha, Amitabha, incessantly, you can also reach this pure thought. As long as it is a pure thought, you can manifest The Pure Land of Ultimate Bliss as well.

So as death approaches us, we rely on the pure thought of reciting Amitabha, Amitabha will then manifest in our thought and escort us to rebirth. Where will we be reborn? We will be reborn into The World of Ultimate Bliss (Sukhāvatī) of our own thoughts. The masters in the past said,

> *Though being reborn is definite,*
> *one actually doesn't go anywhere.*

You did not go anywhere! It is still within the dharma-realm of your "one thought." Yet you are definitely reborn into The World of Ultimate Bliss. Why? The manifestation of your thought is The World of Ultimate Bliss—it is the Amitabha you recite!

This method is extraordinary. It tacitly coincides with the wonderfulness of Dao (Tao). Unknowingly, you enter The World of Ultimate Bliss by reciting Amitabha. This method can indeed help sinful mortals like you and me to be liberated eternally from the reincarnation of birth and death within this one life. The Buddha said to us, we sentient beings with deep, sinful karma can only be liberated by this method of reciting Amitabha. *The Infinite Life Sutra* indicates to us,

> *All people, divine beings, and all sentient beings*
> *of present and future, will all be liberated by this method.*

In conclusion, let me summarize what I have shared here in three points:

- First, a great amount of scientific evidence has revealed to us that the soul definitely exists and reincarnation is definitely real.
- Second, reincarnation is dominated by karma.
- Third, the most remarkable cause and effect in reality is

"Reciting Amitabha is the cause, and becoming a Buddha is the effect."

This method includes this phrase: "Namo Amitabha," which means, "Homage to Amitabha." If you wish to be free from the misery of samsara eternally, you can only rely on reciting Amitabha to be reborn into The Pure Land of Ultimate Bliss (Sukhāvatī). I wish for us all to recite Amitabha conscientiously and be reborn into The Pure Land of Ultimate Bliss together! Thank you everyone!

Namo Amitabha!

ADDITIONAL REMARKS

~ THE LAW of CAUSALITY ~

BY MASTER CHIN KUNG

How can we save people from creating evil karma?
How can we save this turbulent society?
There is nothing more effective
than to promote the education of causality.
To promote this education,
we must understand these five basic rules of causality.

1. CAUSE AND ITS EFFECT
HAPPEN AT DIFFERENT TIMES

From cause to effect needs a period of time, which can be observed in the practice of farming. A melon seedling planted yesterday takes several months before reaching fruition. There is no way it can be harvested in a few days. Likewise, your good deeds might not immediately bring good rewards. It takes time for the good effects to materialize.

If you do a good deed now and immediately receive a good reward, it is not the result of this good deed but of a good karma from your past, which, helped by your current good karma, makes the effect become mature more quickly.

> *The good karma you created in the past is the "cause,"*
> *the good karma that you commit in the present*
> *is the "helping-condition,"*
> *and the current reward is the "effect"*
> *of your past good karma.*

Conversely, if you presently do good deeds, and you don't receive good rewards but beget bad retribution instead, it does not mean that your good deeds will not have good results. It means that your past bad karma has now matured and appeared first.

> *The good deeds that you do in the present*
> *act as a "barrier-condition" for the bad karma of your past;*
> *although the power is not enough to completely prevent*
> *the retribution from coming to fruition,*
> *it can definitely weaken the bad retribution,*
> *so that your bad effect is alleviated.*
> *If it wasn't for the good deeds that you are doing in the present,*
> *the bad retribution would have become worse.*
> *This is the intricate relationship*
> *between "cause, condition, and effect."*

Why Do Evildoers Still Enjoy Fortune?

The reason many people do not believe in causality is because they do not understand this universal law. They see evildoers remain at large and escape prosecution, and even bully others and enjoy fortune, while people who have done good deeds do not receive good rewards, still live in poverty, and suffer bitter retribution and indignity. As a result, they deny the law of causality, thinking that there is no retribution for evil deeds, and no karmic rewards for good deeds. In that case, who would be so foolish as to do good deeds?

It seems true that in today's society, most people think it natural to be selfish and egoistic. We view those who do good deeds as fools because we are too shortsighted to understand the principle that

> *Punishment may come late,*
> *but it will definitely come.*

People who have created big fortune in their past lives, despite having committed many sins in this life, can still be enjoying the fortune that they had accumulated in the past, because they have not used up all their fortune yet. After a decade or two, when their fortune is depleted, the dreadful retribution will appear. So,

> *The law of causality will never go wrong.*

2. CAUSE AND EFFECT RUN THROUGH "THREE TIME PERIODS"

These three time periods are the past, the present, and the future.

Nowadays, scientists have confirmed the existence of reincarnation; past and present lives indeed have their cause and effect. So, as Buddha Dharma states,

> *If you want to know your past lives,*
> *look into your present conditions.*
> *If you want to know your future lives,*
> *look into your present actions.*

Cause and effect correspond to each other. Therefore, if you want to know what causes you have planted in the past, all you need to do is look into the retribution in your current life. If you suffer poverty and illness in this lifetime, then in past lives you must have committed the karma of miserliness and killing.

Likewise, this life will have a causal relationship with future lives too.

As stated above, "If you want to know your future life, look into your present actions." So there is no need to seek help from a fortune teller. If you want to know what will happen in your future, all you need to do is examine what karma you are creating in your current life. If in this life, you create the karma of:

- *Wealth-dāna: Using wealth to help people*
- *Dharma-dāna: Imparting your own knowledge and skills as well as the truth of life and the universe to others*
- *Fearlessness-dāna: Enabling people to be rid of disease, fear, or sorrow*

then in the future you will receive the effects of wealth and wisdom, as well as health and longevity.

According to the time that the retribution manifests, the effect can be divided into four types:

a). Current Life Retribution

The karma is created in this life, and the effects are received in this life. This is called "instant karma" or current life retribution. Typically, this happens when you create extremely good or evil karma by doing considerably good or evil deeds, and therefore you receive the retribution in this lifetime.

> *Understanding this principle,*
> *we can absolutely change our destinies by*
> *repenting our past sins and cultivating good deeds.*

In *Liao Fan's Four Lessons*, the author talks about this kind of situation. People who were meant to be poor with a short lifespan became wealthy and lived for a long time after creating a lot of good karma. People who were meant to be healthy and wealthy became poor and short-lived after creating heavy evil karma.

We must know that the current life's effect is called a "flower-retribution." It is like flowers blooming before a plant bears fruit. The real karmic effect is waiting in future lives, and the severity of this "fruit-retribution" will be even more serious than the "flower-retribution."

b). Next Life's Retribution

The karmic seeds planted in this lifetime will beget retribution in the next life. This is the most common phenomenon.

c). Later Lives Retribution

This means that after creating karma in this life, the retribution is not received in the same lifetime nor the next life, but is received in the third, fourth, or even later lifetimes.

d). Uncertain Time Retribution

The karma you created in this lifetime can receive retribution in any lifetime, depending on what conditions you encounter. If the conditions appear in this lifetime, you will receive the retribution in this life; if the conditions will appear in a future lifetime, then you will not receive the retribution until that life.

3. SMALL CAUSE
RESULTING IN A BIG EFFECT

A tiny cause can turn into a huge effect. It is like a small watermelon seed buried in the dirt growing into many big watermelons which are full of many more watermelon seeds. The adage reads, "Give one and beget ten thousand in return."

Regarding this point, there is a story illustrated in the Buddhist sutras.

The Story of a
Brahmin Elder's Offering

When the Buddha was on Earth, an old servant of a Brahmin elder took some spoiled food out of the house and was preparing to dump it out. The moment she went outside and saw the solemn demeanor of the Buddha, deep and profound respect arose from her heart. She wanted to make an offering to the Buddha, but all she had was the spoiled food in hand. How could she offer it to the noble Buddha? Just as she hesitated, the Buddha began to smile and emit light, and happily used His bowl to scoop up the spoiled food from the old woman's hand.

The Buddha turned His head and told Ananda, "This old woman is wholeheartedly devout. Because of the merit of her sincere offering to a Buddha, in the future, she will have fifteen kalpas, such a long time, to enjoy happiness in heaven. And after the fifteenth kalpa, she would descend into the human realm where she would have the karmic condition of being a monk."

At this time, the old woman's master, a Brahmin elder, happened to walk out of the house. Hearing what the Buddha said, he thought it was very incredible!

The Buddha asked the Brahmin elder, "Have you ever seen other incredible things?" The elder replied, "Yes, one time we had 500 horse-drawn carriages traveling together. Because of the hot weather, we went to find a big tree to enjoy the shade. This big tree could cover all 500 carriages, and there was still extra shade left over. The size of the tree was truly unbelievable!"

The Buddha then asked, "Do you know how big the seed of this great tree was?" The elder replied, "As small as a mustard seed, perhaps." The Buddha said, "That is correct! This is the theory of a small cause creating a large effect."

Maitreya Bodhisattva's Theory

Although the cause of the elderly servant making an offering to the Buddha was very small, it begot a big effect! This principle is based on the speed of the mind, which is way too fast. According to Maitreya Bodhisattva,

> *In the snap of a finger,*
> *there are 3.2 billion hundred thousand thoughts,*
> *each one shapes a form,*
> *and in every form exists consciousness.*

One finger snap contains 320 trillion thoughts; the unit is 100 x 1,000, one hundred thousand; 3.2 billion times one hundred thousand is 320 trillion. In one finger snap, there are 320 trillion thoughts.

In one second, suppose you can snap your fingers three times. 320 trillion times 3, it will become 960 trillion thoughts.

In one second, there are 960 trillion thoughts, and each thought is independent. The frequency of this kind of subtle thought is way too high, so Maitreya Bodhisattva said that each thought is extremely fine and there is no way for us to detect and hold it; it is way too fast!

The speed of thought is so fast that within a very short period of time, myriad seeds are planted in our consciousness, and in the future, their effects will last for a very long time. A good example of cause and effect is the story of Maudgalyāyana, as recorded in the Buddhist sutras.

Tragic Retributions for Kalpas from a Single Action

In the past, Maudgalyāyana had one life where he tried to kill his parents. In that life, both of his parents were blind, and his wife was reluctant to take care of her blind in-laws. She tried various ways to make her husband become resentful of his parents, such as saying bad things to estrange them. Finally, she encouraged her husband to kill his parents, and the husband actually gave rise to the evil intention of killing his own parents!

Following the plan, one day, he took his parents out and brought them to a forest. When they were in the forest, he made his parents believe that robbers came. With a wooden stick that he had prepared, he viciously hit his parents, trying to beat them to death. Unexpectedly, as he was savagely beating them, his parents did not call on him to save them, but shouted for their son to quickly run for his life instead, lest he be harmed by robbers. He was so moved by his parents' unconditional love that his conscience came into play; he knelt down in front of them and repented for his wrongdoings.

Because of this evil karma of intending to kill his own parents, his life was shortened, and upon death he fell into the hell realm, suffering a long period of torture. After leaving hell, he still had to endure the misery of the hungry ghost and animal realms. When he finally reincarnated as a human, he was brutally beaten until his bones were pulverized into pieces in each life for 500 lives.

Even Supernal Power Cannot Overcome Karma

Even in his life as Maudgalyāyana, there was no exception. He followed the Buddha as a disciple, attained arhathood, and became Buddha's number one disciple in supernal power. However, when the karmic condition had matured, he became unable to enter samadhi and use his supernal power. His severe karma remained strong. This is the origin of the saying, "Even supernal power cannot overcome karma."

As a result, he was brutally beaten by a group of heretics until every bone in his body was broken into pieces, and thus he entered nirvana. This story clearly illustrates the principle of a small cause resulting in a big effect. He tried to murder his parents only once in that life. How could it cause such tremendous misery in so many lifetimes?

The reason is because the speed of the mind is way too fast, so even if it is only one evil thought, it results in myriad karmic causes. In that past life, he beat his parents for half an hour. According to Maitreya Bodhisattva's explanation, in a second, if one can snap his fingers three times, then in a second one can plant 960 trillion incidents of extremely evil karma multiplied by 1,800 times for half an hour. The number of evil karmic seeds planted is astonishing!

This extremely evil karma resulted not in just the "flower-retribution"—in which his current life would be shortened and he would be ill—but he also received his "fruit-retribution," being reincarnated into hell in the next life. After finishing the sentence in hell, he was then reincarnated into the animal and hungry ghost realms for the "remainder-retribution." And the next five hundred lifetimes as a human, all ending with his bones beaten into pieces, were still the "remainder-retributions" of this one past evil karma that he had created.

One Aftermath Following Another

From this example, we can see how the severe karma can lead to "the flower," "the fruit," and "the remainder-retributions." It is truly like one aftermath following another, with no end in sight. Seeing how fierce this karmic retribution can be, do you still dare be rebellious and hurt your parents? Do you still dare to commit other bad karmas? "Xi Ci" Chapter in *The Book of Changes (I Ching)*, states:

> *Families that accumulate goodness are sure to have*
> *abundant remainder-auspiciousness,*
> *while families that accumulate evilness are sure to befall*
> *plentiful remainder-misery.*

This statement reveals to us that a family which accumulates good deeds will gain extra prosperity and their future generations will be blessed, while the family that accumulates unwholesomeness will have extra sins and bring disaster to their future generations. This passage is an evident testimony of a small cause resulting in a big effect as well.

Master Yin Guang said that, if there is "remainder-auspiciousness" and "remainder-retribution," there must be "original-auspiciousness" and "original-retribution."

The "original-auspiciousness" refers to the person enjoying the good "fruit-retribution" of his own good karma; the "remainder-auspiciousness" is the fortune that he created, becoming the "remainder-retribution" for his descendants. "Original-retribution" refers to a person suffering the evil effect of his own evil karma; "remainder-retribution" refers to his evil effect passing onto his descendants.

Cultivating the Wisdom to Fear the "Cause"

In addition, we must understand that not only is the effect much bigger than the cause, but the longer it takes for the retribution to take effect, the more grievous the retribution will become; like a debt, the longer it takes to pay back, the more interest there will be. So, after we commit a sin, we must quickly repent and start to do good deeds diligently to lessen the bad karma. Or even better, we should accept the consequences as early as possible to lighten our retribution for a grave sin, so as to avoid severe suffering in the future. Buddhism has a saying,

> *Bodhisattvas fear the cause,*
> *while mortals only fear the effect.*

Bodhisattvas are the "awakened ones" who understand the principle of a small cause resulting in a big effect. They know that after committing sins, the future retribution will be extremely horrific, so they remain vigilant and cautious. They do not dare to create bad karmic causes!

Regarding current bad retribution, bodhisattvas know that it is brought about by the bad karmic seeds of the transgressions of their past lives. They understand that, after taking the retribution, the karma will be paid off.

Because of this understanding, they have no fear—they can calmly accept the retribution and will not give rise to affliction. Bodhisattvas accept retribution as it comes and never create new evil karmas. As a statement in the sutras reads,

> *Let the evil karma be resolved*
> *in accordance with the condition.*
> *Planting no more bad seeds,*
> *we will then not suffer new retribution.*

Mortals are often deluded and bewildered. They only see bad retribution as scary, so they spare no effort to escape retribution. Little do they know,

> *The only way to avoid evil retribution*
> *is to stop creating bad karma.*

When a mortal suffers evil retribution, his affliction will arise. In order to escape evil retribution, he might willingly sacrifice others to benefit himself, thus creating all sorts of evil karmas. After creating new evil karmas, he sees no imminent consequences, so he is not afraid to keep going.

If he continues to create bad karma, the causal effects will become unbearably heavy. This is why Buddhas call us mortals "the lamentable ones."

A mortal who is unaware of causality is constantly afflicted, he will create bad causes and suffer from bad effects. After suffering, more affliction arises in him, and he then creates more bad karma and suffers more again. Such a pattern repeats itself, making him endlessly transmigrate in the suffering sea of samsara.

4. GOOD AND EVIL KARMA
DO NOT OFFSET EACH OTHER

In our world, we often say, "The merits offset the faults"—but this is not true with the law of causality. To do goodness is planting good seeds in our hearts; this is "good cause." To do evilness is planting evil seeds in our hearts; this is "evil cause." Good seeds and evil seeds cannot offset each other. When all conditions are in place, each will have its own effect.

Although good and evil cannot offset each other, they will affect each other. Doing good deeds and planting good causes now is an "assisting condition" to the previous good karma that you had planted; it will increase its effect. And it will also work as a "buffering condition" to the previous bad karma, weakening its effect.

So after your good deeds, if you continue to do good, your previous good causes will receive more and more "assisting conditions." They will become more and more powerful, and the good effects you receive will become better and stronger. Just like "Xi Ci" Chapter in *The Book of Changes* (*I Ching*) denotes:

One will not achieve prestige
if he has not accumulated ample goodness.

A Grave Sin Can Be Given
Light Retribution

Only by accumulating good deeds continuously can a good reputation be realized. Relatively, after doing evil deeds,

149

if you repent and diligently do good deeds, the power of your bad seeds will be weakened little by little, and the evil retribution you receive will be lessened. This is "a grave sin is given light retribution."

There is a very well-known example in history about Master Xuan Zang*, which perfectly interprets this concept. Master Xuan Zang became ill shortly before his death. He suspected that his ailment had something to do with possible mistakes in his translation of Buddhist sutras. That night, Avalokiteśvara Bodhisattva came to his dream, telling him that it was a lightened retribution for his past lives' grave sins; much of the grave karma that he had committed in past lives was eliminated through this one disease due to the merit he had planted by translating Buddhist sutras.

On the other hand, the current evil karma you are creating is an "assisting condition" to the evil seeds of the past, it will strengthen the influences of the evil seeds and weaken the effect of the good seeds that you planted in the past, becoming an obstacle in your life.

---

*Master Xuan Zang, 602–664, Tang Dynasty, was one of the greatest translators in Chinese Buddhism history. He went on a pilgrimage to India between the ages of twenty-eight to forty-three and brought back to China a massive number of Buddhist sutras. Then he spent the rest of his life translating them into Chinese, which had a great impact on Chinese Buddhism and society. Under Emperor Tang Tai Zong's request, he recalled his journey. It was written down by his disciple and became the book of *The Great Tang Records on the Western Regions*. This book has become an important historical document about ancient India. One of the four greatest Chinese novels, *The Journey to the West,* is based on his story.

So after you create evil karma, if you continue to do bad deeds, your previous bad karma will receive more and more assisting-conditions; their power will become stronger and stronger until it reaches what we call "wickedness to the fullest" and finally results in irreversible evil retribution in the future. According to the "Xi Ci" Chapter in *The Book of Changes* (*I Ching*):

> *One will not perish if he does not accumulate evil.*
> *Only by continuing to accumulate evilness*
> *will he cause self-destruction.*

Relatively, after doing good deeds, if you then do a lot of bad deeds, the strength of those good seeds will also be weakened, and the good effects that you receive will become weaker.

Reincarnation:
Difficult to Elevate, Easy to Fall

A book titled *The Statistics of Historic Stories in Causality* tells us that quite a few practitioners in their previous lives had achieved great success. Unfortunately, their achievement was not as good in the following life. This indicates to us that it is difficult to elevate, but to fall downwards is extremely easy. The statistics generated from the stories of the book mentioned above offer us an inference that the horror of the six realms of reincarnation and the relationship between good and evil karmas are indeed worth contemplation.

In fact, the rules of causality are extremely intricate. It is not something that can be explained in just a few words. Even bodhisattvas and arhats* have no way to understand it fully. Only Buddhas can.

5. CAUSALITY IS NOT ILLUSIVE, KARMA WILL NOT BE UNDERMINED

> *Even after hundreds of thousands of kalpas,*
> *the karma created will not vanish;*
> *when the conditions are in place,*
> *the effects will come back upon you.*

The seeds of good and evil that we have planted will fall into the fields of our alaya consciousness. Alaya-vijnana* is like a vast warehouse where the karmic seeds are stored. They will never be lost and will never deteriorate. How troublesome this is!

These seeds have become karmic causes. Even after hundreds of thousands of kalpas, when a long time has passed, once the appropriate conditions are in place, these karmic seeds still manifest their effects, and you will receive the effects. You must wait for the retribution to take effect, because only then can this karma be resolved.

---

*Arhat is a Sanskrit word for one who has gained insight into the true nature of existence and has achieved nirvana. Mahayana Buddhist traditions have used this term for people who advance far along the path of Enlightenment but have not reached full Buddhahood.

*The alaya-vijnana is the foundation or basis of all consciousness, and it contains impressions of all of our past actions. These impressions become "seeds" in our consciousness, and from these seeds, our thoughts, opinions, desires, and attachments grow.

Therefore, as long as we are still within the six realms of reincarnation, we can never escape the cause and effect of our karma. That is why only deluded and bewildered people dare to create bad karma. Awakened bodhisattvas will absolutely not dare to create bad karma, because they understand that the retribution of causality is exceedingly exact.

Can a Buddha Evade the Universal Rule of Causality?

Even after you become a Buddha, you will still receive the retribution of the evil karma that you had created. Shakyamuni Buddha, in His later years, had severe back pain. The pain came from his bad karma in a past life long ago when he was a wrestler. Having been deceived by his opponent twice, he held a grudge in his heart. In one match, he broke his opponent's spine and causing his death.

The extremely vicious deed also resulted in his own life span being shortened, so he died young. Upon death, he fell into hell and endured extreme suffering. After he left hell, he still had the painful "remainder-retribution" for his terrible deed, and when he was back in the human realm, he always had the residual impact of back pain for lifetimes. Even kalpas later, during the lifetime when He became the Buddha, this remainder-retribution was not yet completely resolved, and He still had to suffer the effect of back pain.

The Buddha also demonstrated retribution from other bad causes. His feet were stabbed by splinters from wood chips, which was the remainder-retribution from a previous life when he had used spears to stab other people's feet.

On another occasion, during a three-month summer retreat, the Buddha could only eat the grains meant for feeding horses because the food supply had run dry. That was because, in a past life during the era of Vipassi Buddha, he was a heretic leader; due to his jealousy of Vipassi Buddha receiving people's offerings, he criticized that the Buddha only deserved to eat horse food. The remainder-retribution of this verbal karma caused Shakyamuni Buddha to eat horse food for three months in His life.

When King Virudhaka of Kosala tried to obliterate Shakyamuni Buddha's clan, the Buddha successfully stopped the king's attacks three times but was still unable to change the doomed, disastrous karma of His family. At that time, the Buddha had a headache for three days, because in a past life he had used a stick to beat the head of a big fish three times.

All these tell us that the universal rule of cause and effect is not a falsehood, and even a Buddha cannot avoid it.

Can Sukhāvatī Rebirth Shield Us from Causality?

What about Pure Land practitioners who are reborn in Sukhavati, the Pure Land of the Ultimate Bliss? Does it mean that after being born into Sukhavati, you no longer owe a debt, even if you previously killed someone? Does it mean that you can now avoid paying back your debt?

No, absolutely not!

The effects from a heavy sin may be lightened,
but they can never remain unresolved!

Sukhavati is a very good environment for us to cultivate. It provides us unlimited time to cultivate until we become a Buddha. Amitabha allows us to postpone receiving our bad retribution, but nowhere does the sutra say that our bad karma can be erased—that would be impossible!

Even after we become a Buddha in Sukhavati, when we go to other worlds to liberate all beings, we will still have to deal with the bad effects when our evil karma matures. But by that time, you would have become a Buddha and have crystal clear insight into the retribution of causality. Your heart would remain still as thusness (referring to noumenon, self-nature, true heart, truth, Buddha nature, Dharma body, etc.), you would be liberated and at ease; you would not feel suffering or affliction from the retribution.

As Pure Land practitioners, we also have to eradicate evilness and practice goodness earnestly. Do not have the misconception of thinking that we can have our own way and fear nothing since we have Sukhavati and Amitabha Buddha to rely on. If you become idle and commit bad karma, you will suffer enormous retribution in the future! Because the law of causality is the universal *truth*; it is the law by which the universe runs. This *truth* is not far away; it happens right here in our daily lives. But,

> *He who does not believe in causality*
> *cannot see the causal phenomenon happening around him.*
> *Once he understands the rules and believes in this truth,*
> *he will notice that the retribution of cause and effect*
> *occurs in everything around him.*
> *Everything is correlated with the rule of cause and effect.*

In conclusion, the education of causality can save people's hearts from depravity. The theory of causality is profound and vast. The above is merely a fundamental introduction to the law of cause and effect. Hopefully, it can help everybody understand the basic concept.

AFTERNOTE

—THE METHOD OF RECITING AMITABHA—

Now we know that the endless birth and death of reincarnation is excruciatingly tragic, and the swiftest and best way to be free from samsara is to recite Amitabha. But how? A poem from a contemporary laity, Xia Lian Ju, has divulged to us the best method of reciting Amitabha.

> *Amitabha teaches me to recite Amitabha,*
> *Listen attentively to my own recitation while reciting;*
> *Amitabha, Amitabha... one recitation after the other...*
> *It turns out that Amitabha is reciting Amitabha.*

Our deluded heart is full of scattered thoughts. While chanting, we must focus our attention on this name of Amitabha and pay no attention to our wandering thoughts. By *listening* attentively to our own recitation, we think of nothing, we just *listen* to our own voice. When *listening* clearly and keeping this "pure thought" continuously, we will recover our self-nature little by little—because "Amitabha" is the self-nature, the noumenon, the thusness, the true heart, the *truth*. By reciting the name of Amitabha in remembrance of our own self-nature, along with the inconceivable blessings of Buddha's infinite merits, our self-nature will have no doubt and can be recovered.

> *Ultimately, it turns out that Amitabha is reciting Amitabha.*
> *We have attained the same heart, the same aspirations,*
> *and the same conducts as Amitabha!*
> *We Have Returned to The "ORIGIN"!*

When we find we cannot hear our own recitations, we must increase our vigilance right away and bring our wandering thoughts back to our recitations by *listening* to our own recitation of Amitabha!

This poem tells us to ignore those wandering thoughts and just concentrate on *listening* to our own recitations of Amitabha. Before we know it, our mind will be purified and we will infuse into the Buddha's realm. We will have recovered our own Buddha nature, the self-nature!

The merits of reciting Amitabha are inconceivable!

If you understand the law of cause and effect now, you would believe that

> *"Reciting Amitabha" is the cause, and*
> *"Becoming a Buddha" will be the effect.*

Try it! You will be amazed, just like the people in these links:

A Nice Rendition of Amitabha

https://www.youtube.com/watch?v=J6yyEBXaaK8

- A group of Americans get together to chant Amitabha with their simple instruments for hours once a week. So peaceful! So beautiful!

- They were told that Amitabha is the Buddha of the World of Ultimate Bliss.
  Amitabha has infinite light, infinite life, and infinite merits and wisdom.
- They enjoy chanting Amitabha and contemplate bathing under His light.

Amitabha Buddha in Minutes

https://www.youtube.com/watch?v=g2WwoVN7GPQ&feature=youtu.be

- There are countless Buddhas in the universe.
- Shakyamuni manifested as a Buddha in our world.
- Amitabha is "The King of All Buddhas." The power of His Vows is the greatest and His wisdom is supreme. He created the Western Land of Bliss on your behalf.
- The login password to His blissful land is Namo Amitabha.

What Is the Meaning of Namo Amitabha?

https://www.youtube.com/watch?v=VzBuItn6XF0

- I entrust my life to the awakened one who has infinite light and infinite life.
- All who recite Amitabha will immediately be protected by His blessings and will, in the end, be reborn into His Pure Land, a place that is free from suffering forever.
- In the Pure Land, all will become Buddhas quickly.

Amitabha in America

http://www.purelandbuddhism.org/ea/45

- Once I started reciting Amitabha, my anxiety vanished without a trace.

- Spirits exist after death. When Peter began reciting Amitabha on their behalf, the ghosts and spirits immediately stopped their pestering.
- Amitabha's compassion and power are beyond the imagination of us mortals.
- Many illnesses are related to karma and vengeful spirits. In such instances, it is very hard to cure the disease without liberating the spirits to eliminate the relevant karmic obstructions.
- Amitabha recitation is a rare and precious treasure. People who are fortunate enough to learn it should cherish the opportunity and recite Amitabha as often as they can.

In America, an Auspicious Rebirth

http://www.pureland4:42buddhism.org/ea/337

- Huang Xixun was reborn into the Pure Land, even though he had read very few Buddhist books. He practiced Amitabha recitation for only a short time, was not a vegetarian, and did not take refuge in the Three Gems before he died.
- Although he was told by doctors he had only two or three months left to live due to terminal brain cancer, he lived another year by reciting Amitabha.
- He saw that every page of *The Amitabha Sutra* was full of little images of Amitabha when he was reading the sutra. Later, he dreamt Amitabha came to see him multiple times and said that, He would definitely come to escort him when his time came.
- A bright beam of shifting, multi-colored light suddenly appeared before me (Xixun's wife) and

enveloped Xixun's bed. My eyes were closed, but I could see everything clearly. The Buddha light contained pale-pink, light-purple, gold, and light-blue colors. The strongest, most dazzling color was white. This light resembled the sparkle of the highest-quality diamonds. The entire beam of Buddha light was like an intricately woven pattern, ever-changing and multi-colored.

Amitabha Recitation, City of Ten Thousand Buddhas

http://www.cttbusa.org/amitabha_session/amitabha_session.asp

- The three Pure Land sutras are:
  1. *The Larger Sutra on Amitabha–The Infinite Life Sutra*;
  2. *The Smaller Sutra on Amitabha–The Amitabha Sutra*; and
  3. *The Contemplation of Amitabha Sutra–The Visualization Sutra*.

- Countless kalpas ago, Bhikshu Dharmâkara made forty-eight inconceivable vows in front of Lokêśvararāja Buddha. He vowed that His Buddhaland would be the most blissful and pure, and that all who are born there will not regress until realizing Buddhahood. Bhikshu Dharmâkara is now Amitabha.

- The three lower realms of existence and suffering are not found in Amitabha's Pure Land. The Pure Land of Amitabha is filled with wondrous sounds and adornments.

- The Pure Land practice is to make rebirth to The Land of Ultimate Bliss your mind's essential aim. By keeping this thought foremost at all times, in all places, you will find you have renounced your defiled thoughts and obtained pure thought, because the absence of defiled thoughts is pure thought.

Dying to Be Me! Anita Moorjani at TEDxBayArea

https://www.youtube.com/watch?v=rhcJNJbRJ6U

- I was in a coma. My eyes were closed but I could see everything happening all around my body, not just in the room where my body was, but beyond. I could be everywhere at the same time. It was like wherever I put my awareness, there I was. (The Buddha told us: The consciousness knows no limits, transcends time and space.)

- In this amazing expansive state, I felt like I was in a realm of clarity where I understood everything. I understood that all of us were much greater and more powerful than we realize when we are in our physical body. I also felt that I was connected to everybody. I felt that we all share the same consciousness. (Einstein: Natural and Spiritual, in a Meaningful Unity)

- I didn't want to go back to my sick and dying body. I was a burden to my family, I was suffering. There was no good reason, so I didn't want to go back. But in the next instant, I felt I completely understood—now that I knew what I knew and what caused the cancer, I knew my body would heal very, very quickly if I chose to go back. Within five days, the tumors in my body shrank by 70 percent. After five weeks, I was completely cancer-free and was released from the hospital to go home. (Buddha Dharma: Our world is manifested by our heart and altered by our consciousness.)

- Imagine you are in a warehouse. If you have only a flashlight, you can only see things which are illuminated by your small light. But if there is a big beam of light, you can see everything; it insinuates that so much more exists than what we believe, so much more exists than what we experience. (The Buddhas have completely recovered self-nature; their beam of light is infinite, so their merits, wisdom, and capabilities are infinite. Our flashlight is small now, but it will become bigger once we work on recovering our self-nature; our fortune and wisdom will also grow accordingly.)
- The beam of this light is your awareness. When you flash your awareness on something, it becomes your reality. There can be something else that is right under your nose, but if your flashlight is not shining on it, you won't even notice it. (Confucianism: The greater one's heart is, the more wisdom and fortune he begets.)
- We will have a different life and world if we change our awareness. (The destiny of individuals and nations as well as the world can be changed!)

Namo Amitabha!

Wealth-dāna:
Using wealth to help people, begets wealth.

Dharma-dāna:
Imparting your own knowledge and skills as well as the truth of life and the universe to others, begets wisdom.

Fearlessness-dāna:
Enabling people to be rid of disease, fear, or sorrow, begets health and longevity.

Practicing Dharma-dāna by promoting this book, you are promulgating the truth of life and the universe. And you will obtain immense merits and beget "wisdom."

*All net proceeds from the sales of this book
will be utilized for the work of MahayanaPureland.org
For more copies or e-book, please visit Amazon.com
For more information on related subjects, please visit
MahayanaPureland.org
To contact us, please email us:
team@mahayanapureland.org*

May the merit
accrued from this act
adorn Buddha's Pure Land,
repay the Four Kindnesses above,
and relieve the suffering
of those in the Three Paths below.
May those who see or hear of this
bring forth the heart of
understanding and compassion
and, at the end of this life,
be born together into
The Land of Ultimate Bliss.

Printed in Great Britain
by Amazon